EMPIRICALLY BASED TAXONOMY:

How to Use Syndromes and Profile Types Derived from the CBCL/4-18, TRF, and YSR

Thomas M. Achenbach
Department of Psychiatry
University of Vermont

Ordering Information

This book and all materials related to the Child Behavior Checklist can be ordered from: University Associates in Psychiatry
1 South Prospect St.
Burlington, VT 05401-3456
Fax: 802/656-2602

Proper bibliographic citation for this book:

Achenbach, T.M. (1993). *Empirically based taxonomy: How to use syndromes and profile types derived from the CBCL/4-18, TRF, and YSR.* Burlington, VT: University of Vermont Department of Psychiatry.

Related Books

Achenbach, T.M. (1985). *Assessment and taxonomy of child and adolescent psychopathology.* Newbury Park, CA: Sage Publications.

Achenbach, T.M. (1991). *Integrative guide for the 1991 CBCL/4-18, YSR, and TRF profiles.* Burlington, VT: University of Vermont Department of Psychiatry.

Achenbach, T.M. (1991). *Manual for the Child Behavior Checklist/4-18 and 1991 Profile.* Burlington, VT: University of Vermont Department of Psychiatry.

Achenbach, T.M. (1991). *Manual for the Teacher's Report Form and 1991 Profile.* Burlington, VT: University of Vermont Department of Psychiatry.

Achenbach, T.M. (1991). *Manual for the Youth Self-Report and 1991 Profile.* Burlington, VT: University of Vermont Department of Psychiatry.

Achenbach, T.M. (1992). *Manual for the Child Behavior Checklist/2-3 and 1992 Profile.* Burlington, VT: University of Vermont Department of Psychiatry.

Library of Congress #93-060057   ISBN 0-938565-25-7

Printed in the United States of America 12 11 10 9 8 7 6 5 4 3 2 1

USER QUALIFICATIONS

The Manuals for the Child Behavior Checklist/4-18 (CBCL/4-18), Teacher's Report Form (TRF), and Youth Self-Report (YSR), provide detailed administration and scoring instructions for these instruments. Prospective users should be fully familiar with the appropriate Manual. The *Integrative Guide* presents relations among the syndromes derived from the three instruments and illustrates procedures for coordinating them.

Proper use of the instruments requires knowledge of the theory and methodology of standardized assessment, as well as supervised training in work with children. The training required will differ according to the ways in which the instruments are to be used, but graduate training of at least the Master's degree level is usually necessary.

No amount of training can substitute for professional maturity and a thorough familiarity with the procedures and cautions presented in the Manuals. It is especially important to maintain strict confidentiality of responses and to avoid labeling individuals solely on the basis of scale scores.

PREFACE

In Assessment and Taxonomy of Child and Adolescent Psychopathology (Achenbach, 1985), I laid out some tasks that seemed fundamental to improving our ways of helping troubled children and youth. These tasks were organized around the concepts of *assessment*—identification of the distinguishing features of individual cases—and *taxonomy*— the grouping of cases according to their distinguishing features. In *Empirically Based Assessment of Child and Adolescent Psychopathology: Practical Applications* (Achenbach & McConaughy, 1987), Stephanie McConaughy and I illustrated the use of empirically based procedures to assess a wide variety of behavioral and emotional problems.

The present book deals with the taxonomic aspects of the tasks set out in the two previous books. It is the first publication on the derivation of profile types from cluster analyses of the eight cross-informant syndromes scored from the CBCL/4-18, TRF, and YSR. The profile types provide a basis for taxonomy that takes account of the *patterns* and *elevations* of scores across all eight syndromes. Chapter 5 compares and contrasts the taxonomic use of profile types and individual syndromes, while Chapter 6 reports correlates that have been found for the profile types and syndromes.

The advances in empirically based taxonomy can facilitate research and services in numerous ways. As outlined in Chapters 7 and 8, empirically based taxonomy can be especially helpful in conjunction with an *actuarial strategy* for decision-making. This entails testing predictive relations between assessment data and outcomes for cases grouped according to empirically based taxa. The predictive relations are then applied to decisions about new cases that match the taxa on which the predictive findings were based.

PREFACE

Taxonomic and actuarial notions may seem foreign to some readers. However, this book is intended to demonstrate how they can improve our ways of helping troubled children and youth. Pressures to make services more rational, cost-effective, and accessible to all children argue for using more rigorous, empirically based approaches to taxonomy and decision-making. Potential users include practitioners, researchers, trainees, and administrators in mental health, special education, and related fields.

In referring to new research accomplishments, I have generally used the first person plural "we." This reflects the contribution of the following people to the work reported here: Neil Aguiar, Judy Amour, Janet Arnold, Jill Brown, Chris Chase, Bruce Compas, Craig Edelbrock, Judy Ewell, Catherine Howell, David Jacobowitz, Virginia MacDonald, Stephanie McConaughy, Susan Oakes, Catherine Stanger, Frank Verhulst, and Andrew Weine. I deeply appreciate the help of all these people, plus others who have contributed in various ways. Most of this work has been supported by University Associates in Psychiatry, a nonprofit health services and research corporation of the University of Vermont Department of Psychiatry.

READER'S GUIDE

CONTENTS

Chapter 1
The Role of Taxonomy in Helping Troubled Children and Youth

Taxonomy refers to the grouping of cases or phenomena according to their distinguishing features. A single grouping within a taxonomy is called a *taxon* (plural: *taxa*). The construction of taxonomies can be referred to as a *taxonic* process. In this book, taxonomic terminology is used to avoid the multiple meanings of the more familiar terminology of "classification" and "diagnosis."

The term *classification*, on the one hand, includes all kinds of groupings, such as those that are imposed for the special purposes of particular users, without regard to intrinsic differences between the phenomena classified. Children seen for treatment, for example, may be classified according to whether reimbursement is by Medicaid or private insurance, but this classification is not based on actual characteristics of the children. The term *diagnosis*, on the other hand, carries an aura of clinical authority that connotes more than the grouping of cases according to their distinguishing features. Although diagnosis can also refer to comprehensive case formulations, diagnostic classifications are not necessarily more authoritative than other classifications. In fact, a leading psychiatric diagnostician has defined diagnosis merely as "the medical term for classification" (Guzé, 1978, p. 53).

Unlike the terms classification and diagnosis, taxonomy emphasizes the derivation of groupings from systematic assessment of their distinguishing features. Taxonomies should thus be based on assessment of features that effectively distinguish between cases, and taxonomies should serve users by communicating knowledge about the distinguishing features. A taxonomy should embody current knowledge, but it should also help to advance knowledge by highlighting important similarities and differences between cases.

HELPING CHILDREN AND YOUTH

Taxonomic issues may seem remote from the everyday needs of those who work with children. (For brevity, I will use "children" to include infants and adolescents.) However, taxonomy is relevant to the following aspects of children's services:

1. **Assessment**. To tailor interventions to the needs of each case, we must identify the important distinguishing features of the case. Our notions of what the most important features are and our selection of assessment procedures depend on taxonic assumptions, even if these are not explicitly recognized. Taxonomy thus provides the focus for assessment.

2. **Selecting interventions**. When we select an intervention to change something about a child, family, or situation, our notions of the target for change depend on taxonic assumptions about similarities between the present case and others for which the intervention has been effective.

3. **Training practitioners**. To convey knowledge and improve clinical skills, training must provide differential approaches to cases on the basis of taxonic similarities and differences between the cases.

4. **Administrative classifications**. For administrative purposes such as third party payment and special

educational services, practitioners must often fit children into official classification systems such as the American Psychiatric Association's (1993) *Diagnostic and Statistical Manual* (DSM), the World Health Organization's (1992) *International Classification of Diseases* (ICD), and categories based on Public Law 94-142, the Education of the Handicapped Act (1977, 1981; reauthorized as Public Law 101-476, Individuals with Disabilities Education Act, 1990). Although these administrative classifications were not derived by identifying the distinguishing features of actual cases, they reflect taxonic assumptions about categories of disorders.

5. **Advancing knowledge.** To improve knowledge of the causes, course, and best remedies for psychopathology, we need to group cases for purposes of research. Current taxonic groupings constitute hypotheses about the importance of particular distinguishing features. As these groupings are tested through research, they are likely to be modified in light of more advanced knowledge of what constitutes the most important distinguishing features.

EMPIRICALLY BASED TAXONOMY

Taxonomies can be constructed in various ways and may follow different principles at different stages in the development of a field. In biology, for example, major advances were made in the 18th century when Linnaeus constructed a taxonomy of plant species based on detailed descriptions of botanical structures. Taxonomy based on descriptive similarities was later supplemented by evolutionary and genetic bases for forming groups of similar or related organisms.

Taxonomies often employ a mixture of principles. Medical taxonomies (called *nosologies*) group some disorders together because they are all caused by the same pathogen. Other disorders, however, are grouped together on the basis of descriptive similarities, because the specific causes are unknown—as with many tumors—or because the specific causes are less important than the descriptive features, as with bone fractures.

Some taxonomies are based on theoretical inferences about underlying variables. Anna Freud (1965), for example, proposed that child psychopathology be classified according to inferences about the level of development in libidinal and aggressive drives, ego, superego, regressions, fixations, and conflicts. However, there is little evidence that such inferences can be made reliably or validly.

Modern efforts to construct taxonomies of adult psychopathology date from the 19th century. The most influential system originated with Emil Kraepelin in 1883. Kraepelin assumed that accurate descriptions of disorders would lead to the discovery of a different physical cause for each disorder. Although the particular disorders and principles for classifying them have changed over the last century, current psychiatric nosologies such as the DSM and ICD are descendants of Kraepelin's system.

Early nosologies provided few categories for the behavioral or emotional problems of childhood. Until DSM-II was published in 1968, the only DSM categories were *Adjustment Reaction of Infancy, Childhood, or Adolescence,* and *Schizophrenic Reaction, Childhood Type* (DSM-I; American Psychiatric Association, 1952). Although subsequent editions of the DSM have added categories for childhood disorders, these have been based largely on decisions by the DSM committees, rather than on the assessment of representative samples of children.

In contrast to the theoretical approach proposed by Anna Freud (1965) and the committee approach of the DSM, *empirically based taxonomy* involves assessment of large samples of children to determine what problems actually occur together to form syndromes or other groupings on which to base taxonomy. Empirically based taxonomy is not without a conceptual framework, nor is it necessarily incompatible with particular theoretical approaches or the committee approach of the DSM. Its conceptual framework prescribes the use of standardized procedures to assess features of relevant samples of individuals and quantitative analysis of the assessment data to detect associations among the features in a psychometrically sound fashion. The assessment procedures, features assessed, subject samples, sources of data on the subjects, and methods of analysis may be selected on the basis of theory, hypotheses, or committee work. The results may be similar to or different from the results of other approaches. Furthermore, the results may be more or less useful than results obtained in other ways. These are issues to be addressed throughout the book. However, to set the stage, the hallmarks of empirically based taxonomy can be summarized as follows:

1. It aims to capture in a taxonic system certain useful groupings of features that actually occur in a target population.

2. Standardized procedures are used to assess the distinguishing features of individuals in large samples from the target population.

3. The assessment data are analyzed quantitatively to detect associations among features of the individuals assessed.

4. Taxa are derived from the identified associations among features.

5. New cases can be assigned to the taxa via the standardized assessment procedures that operationally define the taxa.

RELATIONS TO EMPIRICALLY BASED ASSESSMENT

This book is a sequel to a previous book on general issues of assessment, taxonomy, and the relations between them (Achenbach, 1985) and another book that presented practical applications of empirically based assessment (Achenbach & McConaughy, 1987). The previous books illustrated empirical approaches to obtaining data about children's functioning from multiple informants and aggregating the data according to syndromes derived separately from each type of informant. The present book advances from syndromes that were each derived from a single type of informant to *cross-informant taxonomic constructs* that have been derived from multiple informants. These cross-informant constructs, in turn, can be applied to individual children on the basis of assessment data obtained from each type of informant separately and also by combining data from multiple informants.

In Chapters 2, 3, and 4, we will consider a variety of approaches to empirically based taxonomy and the findings emerging from these approaches. Chapter 2 presents conceptual and methodological models for constructing taxonomies. Chapter 3 focuses on the derivation of cross-informant syndromes, while Chapter 4 focuses on profile types that are defined by particular patterns of syndrome scores. As detailed in Chapter 5, our empirically based assessment procedures provide operational definitions of taxa that make it possible to link new cases to previously derived taxonomies in a rigorous fashion. By operationally defining taxa in terms of standardized assessment procedures, users can identify correlates of the taxa and apply the taxa under diverse conditions, as illustrated in Chapters 6 and 7. Chapter 8 provides an overview of the current status and future directions of empirically based taxonomic research and practice.

SUMMARY

Taxonomy involves the derivation of groupings from systematic knowledge of features that distinguish among cases. A taxonomy should embody current knowledge and should help to advance knowledge by highlighting important similarities and differences between cases.

Taxonomy can contribute to helping children by improving assessment, selection of interventions, training of practitioners, use of administrative classifications such as those in the DSM and special education regulations, and understanding of similarities and differences between disorders.

Empirically based taxonomy aims to capture the groupings of features or individuals that actually occur in a particular population. It uses standardized procedures to assess representative samples of the population and derives taxonic groupings from associations among features identified through quantitative analyses of the assessment data.

Empirically based assessment provides operational definitions of taxa that make it possible to link individual cases to taxonomies in a rigorous fashion. The assessment procedures can be applied under diverse conditions to link individuals according to their syndrome scores and according to profile types that reflect particular patterns of syndrome scores.

Chapter 2
Conceptual and
Methodological Models

Classification greatly simplifies the processing of information by chunking things into groups assumed to share certain properties. Without such chunking, we would have to process every detail of every new stimulus as if it were totally unique. This would severely limit our ability to apply knowledge gained from previous stimuli to new instances of similar stimuli.

Classification requires us to abstract certain features of objects that mark them as members of a particular class. In classifying objects, we therefore focus on similarities that define membership in a particular class and differences that distinguish one class from another. Yet, all objects are classifiable in multiple ways, such as by weight, color, or size. Many classifications involve multiple features that are not defined solely by variations in a single physical property. To classify objects as articles of clothing, vehicles, furniture, fruits, vegetables, or animal species, for example, we must abstract and combine multiple features.

THE CLASSICAL MODEL OF CATEGORIES

The traditional view of classification is that it places objects in categories that are defined by certain necessary and sufficient criterial features. In other words, an object is assigned to a category if, and only if, it has all the defining features of the category. Furthermore, all objects that have the defining features of a category are considered to be members of that category. This model thus implies mutually exclusive categories that have clearcut boundaries between them.

THE PROTOTYPE MODEL OF CATEGORIES

In contrast to the classical model, research on cognition has shown that there is considerable fuzziness in the way people actually use categories. Even within familiar categories such as furniture, fruits, and vegetables, the members do not all share the same defining features (Cantor & Genero, 1986). Rugs and lamps, for example, may be categorized as furniture, but they share few features with more typical examples of furniture, such as tables and chairs. Furthermore, there are many borderline cases that share features of multiple categories. Tomatoes, for example, share features with fruits and vegetables that make it difficult for people to classify them as one or the other.

Cognitive research indicates that people do not classify objects according to necessary and sufficient criterial features. Instead, objects are classified according to the *degree to which* they share features that are thought of as belonging to a particular class. Contrary to the fixed set of necessary and sufficient defining features assumed by the classical model, the research evidence indicates that categories are mentally represented by sets of loosely associated features. Because the defining features of a category are not perfectly correlated with each other, not all the defining features of a category are shared by all members of the category.

To take account of the imperfect association among the features representing a category, an alternative to the classical model has been proposed. This is known as the *probabilistic* or *prototype* model (Smith & Medin, 1981). The term "probabilistic" emphasizes that the defining features of a category are not all uniformly present in all cases belonging to the category. Instead, the features tend to be associated with one another only in a correlational, "probabilistic" fashion. The term "prototype" refers to the representation of a category in terms of a set of features that constitute an ideal type. The ideal type, or prototype, is an abstraction that may not be perfectly duplicated by any real cases. Yet, it provides a template with which individual cases can be compared to evaluate their candidacy for category membership.

According to the prototype model, classification is primarily a *quantitative* process which depends on the number of features that an object shares with the prototypic features of a category (Smith & Medin, 1981). Objects that have many features of Category X and few features of any other category are easily placed into Category X, even though they do not have exactly the same features as all other objects placed in Category X. On the other hand, objects having similar proportions of Category X and Category Y features are more difficult to assign to Category X versus Category Y. Objects that are not decisively more like one category than another may thus be borderline cases and should be recognized as such. As Cantor and Genero (1986) put it:

> Category membership is really a matter of degree.
> Each category properly contains a set of members
> arranged along a continuum of fit; there are many
> ways to be a good example of a category and just as
> many ways to barely belong in a category (p. 253).

CONCEPTUAL MODELS FOR TAXONOMIES OF CHILD PSYCHOPATHOLOGY

Cognitive research on how people use categories has opened up new ways of thinking about classification in general. Several studies have shown parallels between mental health workers' judgments of cases according to DSM diagnostic categories and the assignment of objects to categories such as fruits, vegetables, and furniture (Cantor,

Smith, French, & Mezzich, 1980; Horowitz, Post, French, Wallis, & Siegelman, 1981; Horowitz, Wright, Lowenstein, & Parad, 1981). Cantor and Genero (1986) have interpreted the findings as indicating that DSM diagnostic classification resembles everyday classifications of objects in being based on "fuzzy" categories. That is, the DSM categories are fuzzy because they encompass much heterogeneity, they lack criterial features for decisively distinguishing between categories, and they are applied according to the degree to which cases manifest the prototypic features of the categories.

The fuzziness of diagnostic classifications has prompted efforts to improve the use of existing psychiatric categories by making users more aware of the variability within these categories (Genero & Cantor, 1987). However, the lack of firm empirical basis for existing categories of childhood disorders argues against setting them up as even an admittedly fuzzy "gold standard" to which we must learn to conform. Instead, the findings from cognitive research can help to improve our use of empirical data in conceptualizing children's disorders. The prototype model, for example, may not only reflect processes involved in the use of conventional classifications, but may also suggest ways of constructing better taxonomies of child psychopathology. Accordingly, this book applies the cognitive findings to improving our ways of applying current knowledge and to advancing that knowledge.

APPLICATION OF THE PROTOTYPE MODEL TO EMPIRICALLY BASED TAXONOMY

The prototype model was devised to explain findings on how people use existing categories. Yet it may also help in conceptualizing the findings of empirically based taxonic efforts. As outlined in Chapter 1, taxonic groupings can be empirically derived from quantitative associations found among the features of large samples of individuals.

Statistically associated features can thus operationally define each empirically based taxon, just as correlated features define the prototypes of everyday categories.

By statistically deriving taxa, we can determine the actual magnitude of associations among the features of each taxon. Furthermore, we can evaluate the efficacy of different procedures for assigning individual cases to taxa. We can, for example, evaluate the effects of assigning cases on the basis of the *number* of features they share with the empirically derived prototype of a taxon. We can then compare the effects of using the *number* of features with the effects of assigning cases on the basis of a *weighted combination* of features. We can also try other procedures for quantifying the similarity between individuals and prototypes.

The optimal procedures for deriving prototypes and for representing individuals in terms of them are not self-evident. Instead, any taxonomy should be viewed as a provisional means for organizing current knowledge. As such, it provides a stepping stone to further knowledge, subject to revision as we learn more. Yet, because empirically based taxonomy reflects the actual associations among children's problems, it can also suggest theoretical constructs concerning the nature of childhood disorders.

Although no single approach to research or theory is apt to be sufficient for dealing with all of child psychopathology, enough effort has now been invested in empirical approaches to taxonomy to warrant evaluating their potential contribution. Before addressing the results of the empirical efforts in Chapters 3 and 4, let us first consider the main methodological models employed in the empirical efforts.

METHODOLOGICAL MODELS

Thus far, my references to "models" have mainly concerned conceptual models for classification. Although some categories may seem self-evident and intrinsic to the phenomena being classified, it is now clear that the process of classification is complex, often imprecise, and subject to a variety of interpretations. The prototype model embodies a particular interpretation of categories that is based on findings from cognitive research. This model provides a useful way of conceptualizing the findings on child psychopathology that will be our main focus. However, just as the prototype model is not the only way to think about taxonomy, there is no single methodological model for constructing taxonomies of childhood disorders.

From the possible methodological models, I will focus first on factor analysis (and its close cousin, principal components analysis) as a way of identifying features that tend to co-occur to form syndromes. Thereafter, I will consider the use of factor analytic results to define prototypic syndromes, the quantification of syndromal constructs, and tests of the utility of such constructs. In Chapter 4, I will consider the use of cluster analysis to identify groups of individuals who manifest similar profiles of scores across multiple syndromes.

Factor analysis and cluster analysis can be used in many ways. I will emphasize their use in accomplishing the main objective of empirically based taxonomy of child psychopathology, which is to capture the groupings of problems or of individuals that occur in a particular population. To capture such groupings, standardized procedures are used to assess samples of the target population. The data thus obtained are then analyzed to detect associations among problems reported for the samples assessed. When used in this way, factor analysis and cluster analysis function as *descriptive statistics* that do not require major theoretical assumptions. Factor analysis describes the associations among problems in a sample, whereas cluster analysis groups individuals according to similarities in their profiles of scores. These may seem like modest accomplishments. Yet, when we remember that the childhood disorders specified in the DSM and ICD were not derived from direct assessment of representative samples of children, it is clear that systematic description of the problems reported for appropriate samples of children would be a major step forward in the taxonomy of childhood disorders.

Multivariate statistical methods such as factor analysis and cluster analysis can contribute to taxonomy by describing associations among far more problems in much bigger samples than can the unaided human mind. Furthermore, because these methods are quantitatively rigorous, their analytic operations are totally reliable—that is, they always yield the same results from the same input, no matter who carries out the operations (barring clerical errors).

Subjective decisions are involved in choosing sources and procedures for obtaining data, choosing the specific analytic operations, and interpreting the results. Yet the totally reliable analysis of large quantities of data is a major advantage that cannot be duplicated by the unaided human mind. Not only is the unaided mind unable to accurately process multiple variables in large samples, but different people often describe the same input very differently. This severely limits the reliability with which the unaided mind can construct categories of disorders. It probably contributes also to the poor agreement found between clinicians using traditional categories for childhood disorders (e. g., Gould, Shaffer, Rutter, & Sturge, 1988; Mezzich, Mezzich, & Coffman, 1985; Remschmidt, 1988), although somewhat better agreement has been obtained when empirically based assessment instruments were used in conjunction with other data (Rey, Plapp, & Stewart, 1989).

Factor Analysis and Principal Components Analysis

In most applications of factor analysis to the taxonomy of child psychopathology, the initial data consist of scores obtained by a sample of children on a set of features. The scores can be derived from tests, self-reports, ratings by others, and almost anything else that can be quantified. Even qualitative features can be included by scoring them 0 if absent and 1 if present for each child. After each child in a sample has been scored on the features to be analyzed, correlations are computed between every feature and every other feature. The correlations provide a quantitative index of the degree to which the members of each pair of features tend to *covary*—that is, the features have relatively high or relatively low magnitudes in the same individuals.

Principal components analysis (PCA) uses the same general procedure as factor analysis. The main difference is that PCA accepts the initial correlations at face value, whereas factor analysis reduces the correlations on the basis of an estimate of "communality" (the total covariation among all features). The squared multiple correlations among the features are often used to estimate communality prior to factor analyzing the features. PCA and factor analysis may lead to similar conclusions about which items co-occur, especially when more than about 40 variables are analyzed (Snook & Gorsuch, 1989; Velicer & Jackson, 1990a, 1990b). For brevity, I will use "factor analysis" to include PCA, unless otherwise stated.

Correlations computed among all the features provide the actual input for the factor analysis. As implemented by a computer program, factor analysis applies mathematical formulas to the correlations in order to derive "factors." Each factor is like a dimension or vector that consists of *loadings* for all the features analyzed. The loadings are like correlations ranging from -1.00 to +1.00 that show how strongly each feature correlates with the factor.

The computer printout produced by a factor analysis consists of lists of loadings for all features on each factor. The first factor is the one that accounts for the largest percentage of covariation among all the features analyzed. The second factor accounts for the largest percentage of covariation remaining after the effect of the first factor has been subtracted from the correlations among all the features analyzed. The third factor accounts for the largest percentage of covariation after the first and second factors have been subtracted, and so on.

Unless some of the features are perfectly correlated with each other, a factor analysis can produce as many factors as there are features. However, it is usually only the first several factors that reflect substantial covariation among a large number of features. After these "large" factors are subtracted from the correlations among features, most of the remaining factors reflect relatively little covariation among features. Some of these "small" factors reflect mainly the covariation between a single pair of features, while others reflect very weak covariation among larger groups of features.

A set of features having high loadings on a particular factor can be viewed as a *syndrome,* in the sense of features that tend to occur together. In this sense of syndrome, no assumptions are made about whether the covarying features represent a "disease." Instead, "syndrome" is merely used in its original literal sense of a co-occurring group of features. (In its Greek origin, *syndrome* means the act of running together.)

The user of factor analysis can decide how high the loadings should be to qualify features as members of a syndrome. A conventional criterion is that features should load $\geq.30$ to be considered part of a syndrome. The user can also decide how many features must have high loadings on a factor for that factor to be viewed as representing a potentially useful syndrome. The user must make other choices as well, such as the type of factor analysis to employ, the type of "rotation" to apply to the initial factor analytic results, and the number of factors to include in the rotation. (*Rotations* are mathematical transformations of factor analytic results that are intended to approximate *simple structure.* Simple structure is a factor analytic goal in which the number of high loading features on each factor is maximized and the number of factors on which each feature has high loadings is minimized. The aim of simple structure is to identify subsets of closely related features. With respect to taxonomy, the purpose of rotating factors is to construct a relatively small set of syndromes, each of which comprises a maximum number of closely related problems. There are numerous mathematical algorithms for transforming factor analytic results to approximations of simple structure. One of the most popular is the *varimax* rotation, which approximates simple structure by maximizing the variance among item loadings.)

Although the conclusions drawn from factor analyses depend on choices made by the user, the actual derivation of syndromes from the data is mathematically rigorous and perfectly replicable by anyone else using the same data. This is an exceedingly valuable step in the construction of empirically based taxonomies. Other steps must be taken, however, to apply the factor analytic results and to test their utility, as discussed later.

Cluster Analysis of Individuals

Cluster analysis is a statistical method that can be used to identify groups of individuals who have similar scores on multiple features. (As with the other approaches discussed here, even qualitative features can be analyzed if we score them as $0 = absent$ and $1 = present$.) To identify groups of similar individuals, the input to a cluster analysis consists of a set or profile of scores for each individual. The set of scores can consist of scores for many individual features, similar to the feature scores that are subjected to factor analysis. Whereas factor analysis focuses on relations between each pair of features scored for all the subjects, this application of cluster analysis focuses on relations between the profile of scores obtained by each subject and the profile obtained by every other subject.

The first step in cluster analyzing profiles is to compute a measure of similarity between the profiles of every subject in the sample. One commonly used measure of similarity is the *Pearson correlation* (r). When calculated between a pair of profiles, Pearson r indicates the degree to which the profiles have similar *shapes*. (Profile shapes are the patterns of high and low scores, without regard to the precise numerical values of the scores.) Thus, if two profiles have identical shapes, the r between them would be +1.00, even if each of the scores on one profile were much higher than each corresponding score on the other profile.

A second commonly used measure of similarity between profiles is *Euclidean distance*. This is calculated by computing the difference between each of the scores comprising one profile and the corresponding scores comprising the other profile. For example, if two profiles each consist of scales numbered 1 through 8, the difference between Subject A's score on Scale 1 and Subject B's score on Scale 1 would be computed. The same would be done for each of the remaining seven scales. Each difference is then squared and the sum of the squared differences is used as the measure of similarity between the two profiles. In this case, small scores—reflecting small differences between the magnitude of scores on the two profiles—indicate high similarity in the *elevation* of the profiles. Euclidean distance, however, tells us little about similarities between the *shapes* of the profiles.

A third measure of similarity between profiles is the *intraclass correlation* (ICC). Unlike Pearson r—which reflects similarity between the shapes of profiles—or Euclidean distance—which reflects similarity between the elevations of profiles—the ICC reflects similarity between both the *shape* and *elevation* of profiles. In order to obtain the maximum possible ICC of +1.00, two profiles must be identical with respect to both shape and elevation. (For further information on use of the ICC in cluster analysis, see Edelbrock & McLaughlin, 1980.)

Beside the variety of measures for assessing similarity between profiles, there are also numerous algorithms for cluster analysis (Everitt, 1974; Romesburg, 1984). Because cluster analysis has not become as standardized as factor analysis, it is difficult to summarize the common elements of most applications of cluster analysis. Instead, I shall provide details of the approaches employed in our taxonomic research on child psychopathology when the results of this research are discussed in Chapter 4. The aim of these cluster analyses was to create a *typology of individuals* based on similarity between their profiles of syndrome scores. By contrast, the aim of our factor analyses was to identify *syndromes of co-occurring features*. These different multivariate procedures can be meshed together in successive stages of taxonomic research, as illustrated in Chapters 3 and 4.

RELATIONS BETWEEN
CATEGORIES AND QUANTITIES

It is sometimes thought that categorical and quantitative approaches to taxonomy are incompatible with one another. This is not the case. Categories are constructed by human minds as one way of simplifying information. These categories are not inherent in the phenomena themselves. Accordingly, the ways in which we categorize phenomena are affected by how we gather and process data about the phenomena. Quantification can facilitate both the gathering and processing of data, even by scoring qualitative features as *0 = absent* versus *1 = present.*

Because we know too little about the etiology of childhood disorders to construct categories based on specific causes, we need to consider a large variety of potentially relevant data. We also need to experiment with organizing the data in different ways to optimize our taxonic procedures. No one approach is intrinsically correct or optimal for all types of problems at all stages in the advancement of knowledge.

Quantitative Methods for Constructing Categories

Factor analysis and cluster analysis can aid us in experimenting with different ways of organizing large bodies of data. Factor analysis displays its results in terms of dimensions on which features have loadings. Cluster analysis, by contrast, displays its results in terms of groups of similar individuals. We can use the results of a factor analysis to construct categories of disorders by defining categories in terms of the features that load highest on each factor. The results of a cluster analysis of individuals can be used to construct categories of individuals defined by similarities in their profiles of scores. In short, both factor analysis and cluster analysis can be used to construct categories, if desired. Both approaches make use of powerful quantitative operations for detecting the interrelations among features that then offer a variety of taxonic possibilities.

Quantitative Aids to Detecting Categorical Disorders

Instead of starting with quantitative procedures for detecting interrelations among features, suppose we hypothesize that a particular behavioral/emotional disorder exists only in categorical form. Let's call it Schmeisel's Disorder, named for the mythical Professor Heinrich Schmeisel and abbreviated SD. According to our hypothesis, SD involves a neurotransmitter deficit caused by a recessive allele of a particular gene. Only children with the genetically caused neurotransmitter deficit can manifest SD. This implies that children can be clearly categorized as either having SD or not having SD according to whether they have the necessary gene.

Note that our hypothesis about SD is considerably more specific than most current hypotheses about childhood disorders. It posits a specific gene as the cause of a particular neurotransmitter deficit which, in turn, is manifested as SD. It is therefore a better candidate for a categorical approach than are most childhood disorders, for which no such specific hypotheses command much confidence. But we do not know the specific gene locus and we cannot make direct genetic tests. So how do we categorize children into groups of those who do or do not have the gene for SD? And even if we could categorize children according to the gene, would they all manifest SD in the same way? Some disorders having known genetic etiologies, such as Down Syndrome and Prader-Willi syndrome, have a broad range of phenotypic manifestations. Conversely, phenotypic manifestations of such syndromes may be present without the usual genetic abnormality, because other genetic abnormalities may produce similar phenotypes.

Children who have a particular behavioral/emotional disorder are likely to differ with respect to the number and severity of symptoms they display. Some children may have a large number of symptoms while others have few symptoms. Some may have severe versions of certain symptoms while others have mild versions of the same symptoms. The number, severity, and form of the symptoms may vary with the age of the child, as most childhood disorders are not uniformly manifest from infancy through adolescence. The symptoms may also differ with the sex of the child and with other characteristics, such as competencies, vulnerabilities, and environmental stress. Thus, even if we believe that an underlying disorder truly exists in categorical form, the disorder is unlikely to be clearly manifested by identical symptoms in all cases.

If we establish diagnostic criteria that require present-versus-absent judgments of a specific set of symptoms to qualify for a diagnosis of SD, we may miss children who have the disorder but whose symptoms are too mild to be diagnosed as present. On the other hand, we may diagnose some children as having SD when their SD-like symptoms may merely be characteristic of a particular developmental level or have causes other than the SD gene.

To avoid incorrect categorization when the phenotypic boundaries of a disorder are either unknown or variable, quantitative methods such as factor analysis and cluster analysis can be used to determine which symptoms actually tend to occur together. Other quantitative methods can then be used to determine the number and severity of symptoms needed to discriminate between children most likely to have the disorder and those less likely to have it. This can be done separately for groups who may differ in the pattern and severity of their symptoms, such as children of each sex at different ages. The actual procedures for doing this will be presented in Chapters 3 and 4. But the important point is this: Even if a disorder is assumed to occur in a categorical form whereby children either have it or do not have it, the phenotypic manifestations may not always be evident in exactly the same categorical form. Instead, quantitative methods may be needed to detect syndromes of features or groups of individuals that discriminate one disorder from another more clearly than will a categorical criterion specifying a precise set of features, each of which must be diagnosed as present versus absent.

The Use of Quantitative Measures to Form Categories

Beside using multivariate methods to identify groups of features or individuals, we can use the scores on quantitative measures to set boundaries for discriminating between children who are thought to have a disorder and those who are thought not to have it. Whether a quantitative measure is empirically derived by methods such as factor analysis or constructed on the basis of theory, cutpoints can be chosen to minimize misclassifications. Two kinds of misclassification are relevant: *(1) false negatives*—individuals who score on the normal side of the cutpoint but actually have the disorder; and *(2) false positives*—individuals who score on the abnormal side of the cutpoint but do not actually have the disorder. Conversely, the effectiveness of a cutpoint can also be described in terms of the rate of *true positives*, called *sensitivity*—the percent of cases actually having the disorder who score on the abnormal side of the cutpoint; and the rate of *true negatives*, called *specificity*—the percent of cases lacking the disorder who score on the normal side of the cutpoint. Table 2-1 illustrates the relations between false negatives, false positives, sensitivity, and specificity.

In Table 2-1, 100 children were categorized as being either negative for a condition (i.e., normal) or positive for the condition (i.e., abnormal). Starting in the upper left hand box (designated as A), we see that 70 children who were categorized as negative really were negative. These children were the true negatives (TN), in that we have accurately categorized them as negative for the condition. Moving down to *Box C*, we see that 5 children who were actually negative were falsely classified as positive. They were thus false positives (FP).

Looking below the 2 x 2 matrix, we see from A that the true negative rate (also called *specificity*) for our categorization procedure is computed as a percentage of all the children who really were negative. The total n who really were negative is obtained by summing the TN + FP, i.e., 70 + 5 = 75. The true negative rate (specificity) is then obtained by dividing TN/(TN + FP) = 70/75 = 93.3%. Thus, our categorization procedure has correctly identified 93.3% of the normal children as normal. The remaining 5 normal children were incorrectly identified as positive (abnormal), yielding a false positive rate of FP/(TN + FP) = 5/75 = 6.7%.

Moving to the right-hand column of Table 2-1, we see in *Box B* that 10 children who were actually positive for the condition were falsely categorized as negative, designated as FN. In *Box D*, we see that 15 children who were positive for the condition were correctly categorized as positive, designated as TP.

Table 2-1
Relations Between Different Aspects of
Categorization as Normal Versus Abnormal

True Condition

		Negative (normal)	Positive (abnormal)	
Child Categorized as **Negative (normal)**		A. *True Negatives (TN)* $n = 70$	B. *False Negatives (FN)* $n = 10$	$TN + FN = 80$
Positive (abnormal)		C. *False Positives (FP)* $n = 5$	D. *True Positives (TP)* $n = 15$	$FP + TP = 20$
		$TN + FP = 75$	$FN + TP = 25$	$Total = 100$

A. True Negative Rate (Specificity)

= the percent of true normals rightly classified as normal

$$= \frac{TN}{TN + FP} = \frac{70}{75} = 93.3\%$$

B. False Negative Rate

= the percent of true abnormals wrongly classified as normal

$$= \frac{FN}{FN + TP} = \frac{10}{25} = 40\%$$

C. False Positive Rate

= the percent of true normals wrongly classified as abnormal

$$= \frac{FP}{TN + FP} = \frac{5}{75} = 6.7\%$$

D. True Positive Rate (Sensitivity)

= the percent of true abnormals rightly classified as abnormal

$$= \frac{TP}{FN + TP} = \frac{15}{25} = 60\%$$

Looking below the 2 x 2 matrix, we see that the false negative rate is computed as a percentage of children who were really positive, i.e., FN/(FN + TP) = 10/25 = 40%. Below the computation of the false negative rate, we see that the true positive rate (*sensitivity*) is computed as TP/(FN + TP) = 15/25 = 60%. In this example, the true negative rate (*specificity*) of 93.3% is much more favorable than the true positive rate (*sensitivity*) of 60%. Thus, our procedure more accurately identifies children who are negative for the condition than children who are positive for the condition.

Many procedures for assessing physical disorders produce quantitative scores on which cutpoints have been established. People scoring on one side of the cutpoint are considered to be normal, whereas those scoring on the other side are considered to be abnormal, although cutpoints are often adjusted for age, sex, and other characteristics. Examples include measures of blood pressure, heart rate, and cholesterol. The use of quantitative methodology of this sort facilitates categorization of people as having or not having problems such as hypertension and high cholesterol.

Most cutpoints are chosen by making compromises among several considerations. If we set a cutpoint very high at the abnormal end of a scale in order to minimize false positives and maximize specificity, for example, we will automatically raise the rate of false negatives and reduce sensitivity. That is, by counting only the most severely abnormal cases as having the disorder, we may miss milder cases. The high specificity shown in Table 2-1 is a result of using a high cutpoint, which also yields the relatively low sensitivity shown in Table 2-1. On the other hand, if we set the cutpoint at a less extreme score on the scale, we will identify more of the mild cases (minimize false negatives and improve sensitivity), but we will also incur more false positives and reduce specificity. Thus, the sensitivity shown in Table 2-1 could be improved by using a lower cutpoint, but this would increase the false positives, thereby reducing specificity.

The relativistic nature of most cutpoints on measures of problems underlines the fact that the boundaries of disorders are usually fuzzy. The boundaries are affected by multiple factors and are imposed at the discretion of users rather than being inherent in the phenomena that are categorized. Figure 2-1 illustrates the contrasting effects of imposing low versus high cutpoints on the distribution of scores for a disorder. Table 2-2 provides a summary matrix of relations between cutpoints, sensitivity, specificity, false negatives, and false positives in categorizing individuals as having or not having a disorder.

Table 2-2
Relations Between Cutpoints,
Sensitivity, Specificity,
False Negatives, and False Positives

	Low Cutpoint	*High Cutpoint*
Sensitivity	High	Low
Specificity	Low	High
False negatives	Few	Many
False positives	Many	Few

Distributions of Scores and Categorical Phenomena

If we have a quantitative measure of a disorder, the distribution of scores on the measure may take many shapes. Bell-shaped distributions are called "normal" because they are found for many variables. However, measures of pathology tend to yield skewed distributions, with most people obtaining low scores for problems and progressively fewer people obtaining scores in the middle and upper ranges. It is sometimes thought that a bimodal distribution

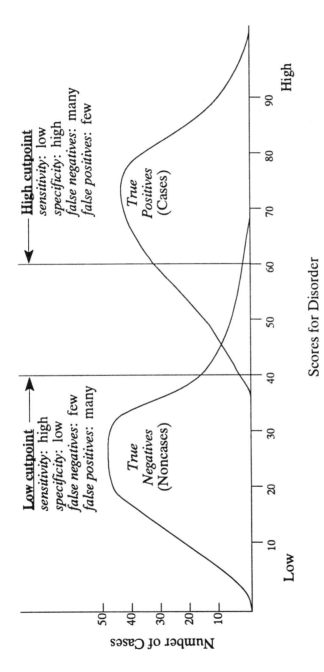

Figure 2-1. Effects of imposing low versus high cutpoints on the distribution of scores for a disorder.

of scores on a measure of pathology reflects an underlying disorder that exists in categorical form. In other words, if some individuals are clustered around one point in the distribution while others are clustered around a second point, one group is assumed to have the underlying disorder whereas the other group is assumed not to have the disorder.

A bimodal distribution may indeed facilitate selection of cutpoints. However, Grayson (1987) has shown that bimodal distributions can arise in many ways, even if the underlying disorder is not categorical. If certain subsets of symptoms on a scale are highly correlated with one another, for example, subgroups of individuals will have similar scores depending on their manifestation of each subset of symptoms. For example, if 40% of the symptom features on the scale are moderately intercorrelated and represent a mild degree of a disorder, the scores of individuals having a mild version of the disorder will cluster around one point at the mild end of the scale. If another 40% of the symptom features are highly intercorrelated and represent a severe degree of the disorder, the scores of individuals having a severe version of the disorder will cluster around a point at the severe end of the scale.

A truly categorical disorder can, of course, yield a bimodal pattern of scores. Yet, such a pattern does not prove that a disorder exists in a purely categorical, present-versus-absent form. Furthermore, even if bimodality is the result of a categorical disorder, the bimodality will seldom be perfect. That is, not all individuals having the disorder will obtain one score while all individuals lacking the disorder obtain a different score. Because there are always apt to be errors of measurement, as well as factors that affect the expression of a disorder, even the bimodal distribution arising from a categorical disorder is apt to have scores above, below, and between the modes. Quantitative methods are thus not incompatible with categorical conceptual models for disorders. Instead, even very strong assumptions about the categorical nature of disorders—such as our hypothetical example of Schmeisel's Disorder (SD)—necessitate appropriate quantitative methods.

QUANTIFICATION AND TAXONOMY

As I argued in the preceding sections, the use of quantitative methods to aggregate and analyze data should not be confused with theoretical commitments to categorical versus noncategorical conceptual models for psychopathology. Categories of disorders can be constructed via multivariate methods to detect syndromes of co-occurring problems and groups of individuals manifesting similar profiles, as well as via cutpoints on distributions of scores. However, at our present stage of knowledge, we are apt to lose valuable information if we prematurely impose rigid borders between one hypothesized disorder and another or between the normal and abnormal. Instead, we must be aware of the relativistic nature of any borders we select. Such borders require decisions about what to include and what to exclude from a taxon. We should therefore assess the tradeoffs in what is gained and what is lost by various means of discriminating between disorders.

Another consideration in relations between quantification and taxonomy is whether quantification is used to indicate the severity of a disorder or the certainty with which a disorder matches a particular prototype. In the cognitive research on prototypes, the number of prototypic features manifested by an object is an index of how similar the object is to the prototype defining a particular category. However, when we are concerned not only with the resemblance of a disorder to a category, but also with the severity of the disorder, the number of features (or symptoms) may be an index of severity. We will address these different functions of quantification in subsequent chapters.

SUMMARY

Classification into categories simplifies the processing of information by abstracting certain features of objects in order to chunk them into groups. According to the classical model of categorization, objects are assigned to mutually exclusive categories on the basis of necessary and sufficient defining features.

In contrast to the classical model, cognitive research has shown that people do not actually categorize objects according to necessary and sufficient criterial features. Instead, objects are categorized according to the *degree to which* they manifest the imperfectly correlated features that define a category. According to the *prototype model*, categorization is a *quantitative* process that depends on the number of features an object shares with the prototype of a category.

The prototype model can aid in conceptualizing the findings of empirically based taxonic efforts. Like the prototypic features that define conceptual categories, features found to be statistically associated with one another can be used to operationally define taxa.

Beside the classical and prototype models for conceptualizing categories, we considered methodological models for aggregating and analyzing data relevant to the taxonomy of child psychopathology. *Factor analysis* and *principal components analysis* can be used to identify syndromes of co-occurring features in samples of children from particular populations. *Cluster analysis* can be used to identify groups of children who have similar profiles of scores.

Categorical and quantitative approaches to taxonomy are not necessarily incompatible with each other. On the contrary, both can make use of similar quantitative methods for identifying co-occurring features with which to define disorders. Both can also make use of quantitative measures for assessing the degree to which children manifest the defining features of a syndrome, as well as cutpoints for discriminating between children who are considered to be in the normal versus clinical range. When used in conjunction with either categorical or quantitative concepts of disorders, the effectiveness of cutpoints can be evaluated according to the percent of *false negatives, false positives, true positives (sensitivity),* and *true negatives (specificity)* they yield in relation to an external criterion.

It is sometimes assumed that a bimodal distribution of scores indicates an underlying disorder that is categorically present or absent. This is not necessarily the case, because bimodal distributions can occur for other reasons as well.

The use of quantitative methods to aggregate and analyze data should not be confused with theoretical commitments to categorical versus noncategorical conceptual models for psychopathology. We are apt to lose valuable information about the actual form of children's disorders if we prematurely impose rigid borders between putative disorders or between the normal and clinical. All borders are relativistic—that is, they involve tradeoffs between particular advantages and disadvantages which should be explicitly evaluated.

Chapter 3
Empirically Based Syndromes

Chapter 2 presented parallels between the *prototype model* for conceptualizing categories and *factor analytically derived* syndromes of co-occurring features. Prototypes consist of features assumed to be correlated with each other, whereas factor analysis derives syndromes from the actual correlations between features found in samples of individuals. These empirically based syndromes represent categories of co-occurring features, but not necessarily categories of individuals.

A category of individuals may be constructed by grouping together those who manifest many features of a particular syndrome. Yet it is also possible for the same individual to manifest the features of more than one syndrome. Thus, for example, the same individual may simultaneously manifest the syndromes of several organic disorders, such as measles, a head cold, and cancer. Each syndrome consists of features that tend to co-occur, but individuals vary with respect to the number of features they manifest from each syndrome. Deriving syndromes is therefore different from deriving typologies of individuals. Both are taxonic enterprises, however, that may shed light on children's disorders in different ways. This chapter deals with the empirical derivation of syndromes from parent-ratings on the Child Behavior Checklist for Ages 4-18 (CBCL/4-18), teacher-ratings on the Teacher's Report Form (TRF), and self-ratings on the Youth-Self Report (YSR) (Achenbach, 1991b, 1991c, 1991d).

I will focus mainly on findings from principal components analyses (PCA) of similar pools of problem items rated by parents, teachers, and adolescents. Variations in the samples of subjects and the people who rate them, errors of measurement, and semantic aspects of the items can all shape the syndromes obtained from a particular pool of items. Furthermore, the pool of items, the subject sample, and the type of rater all constrain the syndromes that can be found. This is because a syndrome cannot be found unless the data include variations in the scores for the relevant features in the sample that is analyzed. On the other hand, different syndromes may be identifiable by other analytic methods applied to other samples assessed in different ways. Nevertheless, by comparing results from analyses of different samples, we can identify *core syndromes* that are relatively consistent despite sampling fluctuations. These core syndromes provide a basis for particular taxonic constructs, although taxonic constructs can also be formed in other ways, as well. The constructs based on core syndromes are not expected to represent all possible childhood disorders. For example, disorders such as autism involve features that are too rare to be detected in syndromes derived from large samples of children.

Syndromes may differ according to such variables as the age and sex of the subjects, as well as the type of informants who rate the subjects. It is therefore essential to examine findings obtained from different informants for children of each sex at different ages before drawing conclusions about the consistency of syndromes across age, sex, and informant. The following sections outline our procedures for deriving core syndromes from the CBCL/4-18, TRF, and YSR, and *cross-informant syndrome constructs* common to these instruments.

CORE SYNDROMES DERIVED FROM THE CBCL/4-18, TRF, AND YSR

Prior to 1991, the syndrome scales derived from the CBCL/4-18, TRF, and YSR consisted of the specific sets of problem items found to load together in separate PCAs of each sex/age group scored by each type of informant (Achenbach & Edelbrock, 1983, 1986, 1987). Some syndromes, such as one designated as *Somatic Complaints*, had counterparts in all sex/age groups, as assessed by parent-, teacher-, and self-ratings. Other syndromes were found for only some of the sex/age groups or in ratings by only one type of informant.

The syndrome scales consisting of items found to load together in a particular set of ratings reflected variations among the patterns of problems seen by each type of informant rating each sex within each age range. However, even within a particular instrument, such as the CBCL/4-18, sex and age differences among the scales hindered comparisons of scale scores obtained by boys versus girls and by different age groups. The age variations also hindered comparisons of scores obtained by the same child at different ages. Furthermore, the variations in syndrome scales across the three instruments made it difficult to compare data obtained from multiple informants rating the same child.

To identify the common elements of syndromes that are found for both sexes in multiple age ranges, we performed new analyses of 4,455 CBCLs, 2,815 TRFs, and 1,272 YSRs completed for children who had been referred for mental health services (Achenbach, 1991a, 1991b, 1991c, 1991d). To avoid biases associated with individual settings, the CBCLs were obtained from 52 settings, the TRFs from 58 settings, and the YSRs from 26 settings. As with the pre-1991 analyses, separate PCAs with varimax rotations were performed for each sex within particular age ranges. The age ranges for the CBCL/4-18 were 4-5, 6-11, and 12-18 years. For the TRF, they were 5-11 and 12-18 years. And for the YSR, the age range was 11-18 years. (Although separate analyses were performed on CBCLs for 4-5-year-olds and 6-11-year-olds, these two age groups were combined in the final syndrome scales for scoring the CBCL.)

Goals of the 1991 Analyses

The 1991 analyses had three main goals. One goal was to identify syndromes that were evident in a majority of the sex/age groups analyzed on each instrument. The common elements of these syndromes would be used to construct *core syndromes* to represent patterns of problems that co-occur for both sexes and different ages, according to either parent-, teacher-, or self-ratings.

A second goal of the 1991 analyses was to identify syndromes that were specific to particular sex/age groups as scored on a particular instrument, as had been done in the pre-1991 analyses. To accomplish these goals, all problem items were analyzed except some of those that were reported for <5% of clinically referred children in a particular sex/age group on a particular instrument. (A few items that were reported for <5% of a particular sex/age group were retained for analysis if they had loaded ≥.30 on syndromes previously derived from multiple sex/age groups.) These item sets will be called the *all-item sets*, which differed somewhat among the three instruments.

A third goal of the 1991 analyses was to construct cross-informant syndromes to represent the common elements of core syndromes that had counterparts in the CBCL/4-18, TRF, and YSR. To achieve this goal, a second PCA was performed on the problem ratings for each sex/age group on each instrument. Unlike the analyses of the all-item sets, these analyses included only the 89 items that have close counterparts on the CBCL/4-18, TRF, and YSR. These item sets will be referred to as the *common-item sets*. The analyses of the common-item sets were designed to detect only those syndromal patterns that were potentially detectible in ratings by all three types of informants. By contrast, the analyses of the all-item sets might detect syndromes restricted to one type of informant. Figure 3-1 summarizes the steps involved in deriving core syndromes, cross-informant constructs, and scales for scoring them.

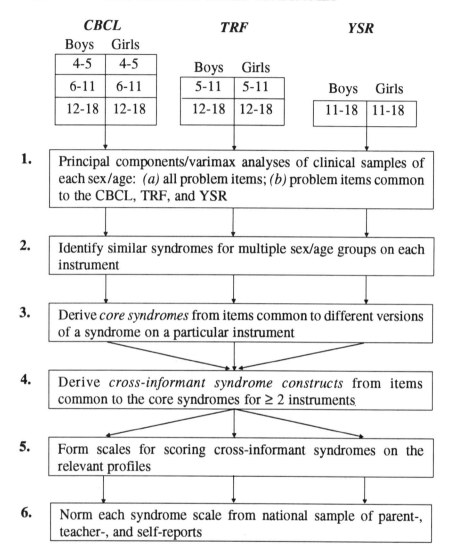

Figure 3-1. Summary of steps in developing syndrome scales that are common to the 1991 profiles for the CBCL, TRF, and YSR.

Procedure for Deriving Core Syndromes

The largest 7 to 15 principal components obtained from the analysis of each sex/age group on a particular instrument were rotated to the varimax criterion for simple structure. The 7- to 15-component rotations were then examined to identify subsets of items that consistently grouped together with high loadings on a rotated component. Four to five rotations were selected that included representative versions of these components. The items loading ≥.30 on these rotated components were then listed side-by-side to identify the version of each component that included the maximum number of high loading items which also loaded highly on the other versions. (Because the syndrome designated as *Aggressive Behavior* included an exceptionally large number of high loading items, only the items loading ≥.40 were retained for the various versions of this syndrome. However, if an item that loaded ≥.40 on the Aggressive Behavior syndrome also loaded ≥.30 on a second syndrome, the item was retained only for the second syndrome.)

After selecting the two to three best versions of each syndrome, we identified the rotation that included the largest proportion of the best versions of each syndrome. (The "best" versions of a syndrome were those that included the largest proportion of items that loaded ≥.30 in most versions of the syndrome.) The versions of the syndromes found in this rotation were retained to represent the sex/age group for which the analysis was done. The manuals for the CBCL/4-18, TRF, and YSR provide illustrations of how specific subsets of items were identified to define particular syndromes for each sex/age group (Achenbach, 1991b, 1991c, 1991d).

To identify core syndromes that underlay the various versions of a particular syndrome, we printed side-by-side lists of the items included in the version of a syndrome obtained from each sex/age group in the analyses of the all-item set. We also printed side-by-side lists of the items included in the versions of the syndrome obtained from each sex/age group in the analyses of the common-item set. A syndrome designated as *Anxious/Depressed*, for example, was found for all sex/age groups in parent-, teacher-, and self-ratings. An item was counted as present in the Anxious/Depressed syndrome for a particular sex/age group if it was found in either the all-item or common-item version of the syndrome for that group. We then determined which items were found in versions of the syndrome for a majority of the sex/age groups on a particular instrument. On the CBCL/4-18, for example, there were six sex/age groups (boys and girls at ages 4-5, 6-11, and 12-18). To be retained for the Anxious/Depressed core syndrome from the CBCL, an item had to be present in all-item or common-item versions of the Anxious/Depressed syndrome found for at least four of the six sex/age groups.

The core syndromes derived from each instrument provided the items for the syndrome scales scored from that instrument. In addition, the core syndromes from the three instruments were compared with respect to the 89 common items in order to identify syndromes whose items were similar in two or more instruments, as described in the following section.

CROSS-INFORMANT SYNDROME CONSTRUCTS

When we compared the core syndromes that were derived separately from the CBCL/4-18, TRF, and YSR, we found eight that had counterparts in at least two of the three instruments. These syndromes were designated as *Aggressive Behavior, Anxious/Depressed, Attention Problems, Delinquent Behavior, Social Problems, Somatic Complaints, Thought Problems,* and *Withdrawn.* Versions of seven of the syndromes were found in analyses of all three instruments but a clear counterpart of the Withdrawn syndrome was not found in the YSR analyses.

To form *cross-informant syndrome constructs* representing the common elements of the core syndromes, we made
side-by-side lists of the items that comprised each core
syndrome. We then identified items that were common to
the versions of the core syndromes derived from at least two
of the three instruments. These items were used to define the
cross-informant syndrome constructs.

After identifying the common items with which to define
the cross-informant constructs, we constructed scales for
scoring each construct from the items of the CBCL/4-18,
TRF, and YSR. These scales operationally define each
construct in terms of the specific scores obtained on the
items of the CBCL/4-18, TRF, or YSR completed by the
appropriate kind of informant.

Instrument-Specific Items

In addition to the items that define the cross-informant
constructs, some items had high loadings on the versions of
a syndrome derived from only one instrument. Some, but not
all, of these items appear on only one instrument. For
example, the item *Disrupts class discipline* obtained high
loadings on enough TRF versions of the Aggressive Behavior syndrome to qualify for the core Aggressive Behavior
syndrome derived from the TRF. Because this item does not
appear on the CBCL or YSR, it could not be included in a
cross-informant construct. However, because it was strongly
associated with the TRF version of the Aggressive Behavior
syndrome, it was retained for the TRF Aggressive Behavior
scale.

A few items that have counterparts on more than one
instrument obtained high loadings on versions of a syndrome
derived from only one of the instruments. An example is
Deliberately harms self or attempts suicide. This item has
counterparts on all three instruments, but it loaded only on
the Anxious/Depressed syndrome derived from the YSR.
Because this item was strongly associated with the YSR

version of the Anxious/Depressed syndrome, it is included in the Anxious/Depressed scale scored from the YSR. Table 3-1 lists the items that define each cross-informant syndrome construct, plus the items that are included in the instrument-specific versions of the syndromes.

Syndromes Specific to the CBCL/4-18 and YSR

The inclusion of instrument-specific items on some of the scales for scoring the cross-informant syndromes captures some of the variations in patterns of children's problems as seen by different informants. Two syndromes that were found in ratings by only one type of informant were also retained for scoring by that type of informant. One of these syndromes, designated as *Sex Problems*, was found in parents' CBCL ratings of 4-11-year-old boys and girls. The second syndrome, designated as *Self-Destructive/Identity Problems*, was found in boys' YSR ratings. Although these two syndromes do not provide a basis for cross-informant taxa, they can supplement the cross-informant taxa by providing a more differentiated taxonomy of problems as seen by parents and adolescent boys.

Norming the Syndrome Scales

To provide a basis for determining the degree of deviance indicated by a child's score on each syndrome scale, we derived norms from 2,368 CBCLs, 1,391 TRFs, and 1,315 YSRs completed for a national sample of children who had not received mental health services within the preceding 12 months (Achenbach, 1991b, 1991c, 1991d). Normalized T scores were assigned to the distributions of raw scale scores on each syndrome scale, separately for each sex at ages 4-11 and 12-18 on the CBCL, ages 5-11 and 12-18 on the TRF, and ages 11-18 on the YSR. Hand-scored and computer-scored profiles display the distributions of T scores, raw scores, and percentiles based on the normative

Table 3-1
Items Defining the Cross-Informant Syndrome Constructs,
plus Items Specific to the CBCL, YSR, and TRF
Syndrome Scales[a]

Withdrawn	*Anxious/Depressed*
42. Would rather be alone	12. Lonely
65. Refuses to talk	14. Cries a lot
69. Secretive	31. Fears impulses
75. Shy, timid	32. Needs to be perfect
80. Stares blankly[b]	33. Feels unloved
88. Sulks[b]	34. Feels persecuted
102. Underactive	35. Feels worthless
103. Unhappy, sad, depressed	45. Nervous, tense
111. Withdrawn	50. Fearful, anxious
	52. Feels too guilty
Somatic Complaints	71. Self-conscious
51. Feels dizzy	89. Suspicious
54. Overtired	103. Unhappy, sad, depressed
56a. Aches, pains	112. Worries
56b. Headaches	**Specific to YSR**
56c. Nausea	18. Harms self
56d. Eye problems	91. Thinks about suicide
56e. Rashes, skin problems	**Specific to TRF**
56f. Stomachaches	47. Overconforms[b,c]
56g. Vomiting	81. Hurt when criticized[b,c]
	106. Anxious to please[b,c]
	108. Afraid of mistakes[b,c]

[a]Items are designated by the numbers they bear on the CBCL, YSR, and TRF and summaries of their content. [b]Not on YSR. [c]Not on CBCL. [d]Not on TRF. (Achenbach, 1991a.)

Table 3-1 (cont.)

Social Problems
1. Acts too young
11. Too dependent
25. Doesn't get along w. peers
38. Gets teased
48. Not liked by peers
62. Clumsy
64. Prefers younger kids
    Specific to CBCL
55. Overweight
    Specific to YSR
111. Withdrawn
    Specific to TRF
12. Lonely
14. Cries
33. Feels unloved
34. Feels persecuted
35. Feels worthless
36. Accident prone

Thought Problems
9. Can't get mind off
   thoughts
40. Hears things
66. Repeats acts
70. Sees things
84. Strange behavior
85. Strange ideas
    Specific to CBCL
80. Stares blankly[b]

Thought Problems (cont.)
   Specific to TRF
18. Harms self
29. Fears
   Specific to YSR
83. Stores up things

Attention Problems
1. Acts too young
8. Can't concentrate
10. Can't sit still
13. Confused
17. Daydreams
41. Impulsive
45. Nervous, tense
61. Poor school work
62. Clumsy
80. Stares blankly[b]
    Specific to CBCL
46. Twitches
    Specific to TRF
2. Hums, odd noises[b,c]
4. Fails to finish[b,c]
15. Fidgets[b,c]
22. Difficulty w.
    directions[b,c]
49. Difficulty learning[b,c]
60. Apathetic[b,c]
72. Messy work[b,c]
78. Inattentive[b,c]
92. Underachieving[b,c]
100. Fails to carry out tasks[b,c]

[a]Items are designated by the numbers they bear on the CBCL, YSR, and TRF and summaries of their content. [b]Not on YSR. [c]Not on CBCL. [d]Not on TRF.

Table 3-1 (cont.)

Delinquent Behavior	Aggressive Behavior (cont.)
26. Lacks guilt	23. Disobedient at school
39. Bad companions	27. Jealous
43. Lies	37. Fights
63. Prefers older kids	57. Attacks people
67. Runs away from home[d]	68. Screams
72. Sets fires[d]	74. Shows off
81. Steals at home[d]	86. Stubborn, irritable
82. Steals outside home	87. Sudden mood changes
90. Swearing, obscenity	93. Talks too much
101. Truancy	94. Teases
105. Alcohol, drugs	95. Temper tantrums
Specific to CBCL	97. Threatens
96. Thinks about sex too much	104. Loud
	Specific to CBCL
106. Vandalism[b,d]	22. Disobedient at home[d]
Specific to TRF	**Specific to TRF**
98. Tardy[b,c]	6. Defiant[b,c]
	24. Disturbs others[b,c]
Aggressive Behavior	53. Talks out of turn[b,c]
3. Argues	67. Disrupts class[b,c]
7. Brags	76. Explosive[b,c]
16. Mean to others	77. Easily frustrated[b,c]
19. Demands attention	
20. Destroys own things	
21. Destroys others' things	

[a]Items are designated by the numbers they bear on the CBCL, YSR, and TRF and summaries of their content. [b]Not on YSR. [c]Not on CBCL. [d]Not on TRF.

samples for each instrument. A child's score on each syndrome rated by each type of informant can thus be quantitatively compared with scores for normative samples of peers, as rated by the same type of informant. In addition, cutpoints on each syndrome indicate a normal range (T scores <67), borderline clinical range (T scores 67 to 70), and clinical range (T scores >70). These cutpoints are indicated by broken lines printed across the profiles. Figure 3-2 illustrates a computer-scored CBCL profile completed for a 15-year-old girl named Ginny. As Figure 3-2 shows, Ginny obtained scores in the clinical range (above the top broken line) on the Social Problems syndrome. Her scores on the other syndrome scales were in the borderline range (between the broken lines) or in the normal range (below the bottom broken line). The TRF and YSR profiles have similar layouts but include items that are specific to their versions of the syndrome scales, plus normative distributions of scores derived from teacher- and self-ratings, respectively.

INTERNALIZING AND EXTERNALIZING GROUPINGS OF SYNDROMES

Notice in Figure 3-2 the heading *Internalizing* on the left side at the top of the profile. The Internalizing grouping encompasses the following syndromes: *I. Withdrawn, II. Somatic Complaints,* and *III. Anxious/Depressed.* On the right side of the top of the profile is the heading *Externalizing,* which encompasses the following syndromes: *VII. Delinquent Behavior* and *VIII. Aggressive Behavior.* These groupings resulted from efforts to determine whether some of the eight cross-informant syndromes were more closely associated with each other than with the other syndromes.

To identify groupings of syndrome scales that covary most closely, we factor analyzed the correlations among the eight syndrome scales. (Factor analyzing correlations among scales that were themselves the results of factor analyses is

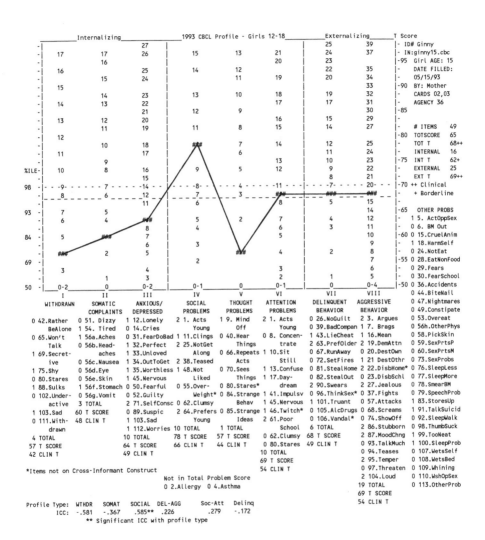

Figure 3-2. Computer-scored CBCL profile for 15-year-old Ginny. Intraclass correlations (ICC) between Ginny's profile and the types derived from cluster analyses are displayed in the lower left corner of the printout (explained in Chapters 4-5).

called *second-order factor analysis*; the factor analysis or principal components analysis of correlations among items is called *first-order analysis*.)

We performed separate second-order factor analyses of the correlations among syndrome scales for each sex/age group scored on the CBCL, TRF, and YSR (Achenbach, 1991a). The largest two factors in each solution were then rotated to the varimax criterion. Thereafter, we computed the mean loading obtained by each of the eight syndromes on the two second-order factors across all sex/age groups on all three instruments.

The Withdrawn, Somatic Complaints, and Anxious/ Depressed syndromes had the highest mean loadings on one second-order factor, whereas the Delinquent Behavior and Aggressive Behavior syndromes had the highest mean loadings on the other second-order factor. These groupings of syndromes reflect a broad distinction that has been called not only Internalizing versus Externalizing (Achenbach, 1966), but also Personality Problem versus Conduct Problem (Peterson, 1961), Inhibition versus Aggression (Miller, 1967), and Overcontrolled versus Undercontrolled (Achenbach & Edelbrock, 1978).

To score individual children for Internalizing and Externalizing, the scores of the items from the constituent syndromes are summed. The scoring profiles provide T scores that compare a child's Internalizing scores and Externalizing scores with those obtained by normative samples of the same sex and age scored by the same type of informant. For example, in Figure 3-2, Ginny's Internalizing and Externalizing raw scores and T scores are printed to the right of her profile. These scores may be used to identify children who manifest problems primarily from one grouping or the other. This can be helpful for making decisions about individual children, such as assignment to particular residential treatment programs, and for research to determine whether there are etiological factors common to the syndromes that form the two groupings. However, the syndromes themselves are likely to provide more differentiated data than the Internalizing-Externalizing distinction, both in the assessment of individual children and in research.

APPLICATIONS OF CROSS-INFORMANT SYNDROME CONSTRUCTS TO TAXONOMY

The analyses outlined in the foregoing sections yielded syndromes of problems that tend to co-occur in ratings by parents, teachers, and youths. The scales and profiles constructed from the syndromes provide standardized ways to describe children's problems as seen by different informants and to compare what those informants report for a particular child with what similar informants report for large normative samples of children. As standardized and quantified descriptions, the scales have many practical and research applications.

In addition to their use as standardized descriptions, the empirically derived cross-informant syndromes also provide a basis for grouping children according to similarities in the problems they manifest. Such groupings can serve a variety of functions. To advance knowledge of children's problems, children who are deviant on one syndrome can be compared to children who are deviant on a different syndrome in order to identify possible differences in the etiology, course, responsiveness to treatment, outcome, and other correlates of their problems. If such differences are found, they would contribute knowledge that can then be used to theorize about the nature and causes of disorders represented by the syndromes, the selection of preventive and therapeutic interventions, and the determination of prognoses for new cases. For example, children whose profiles are deviant primarily on the Social Problems syndrome, like Ginny's profile in Figure 3-2, can be compared to children whose profiles are deviant on a different syndrome, such as Withdrawn, with respect to responsiveness to social skills training.

Findings about the syndromes are likely to keep growing in both scope and detail. Current knowledge about each syndrome is therefore less extensive than it will eventually become. Nevertheless, even in the absence of complete knowledge, the syndromes provide foci for obtaining and organizing assessment data, developing hypotheses, preparing diagnostic formulations, and evaluating outcomes for individual cases. In addition, the syndromes provide an empirical basis for matching individual cases to nosologies, such as the DSM, and special education classifications, such as prescribed by P.L. 94-142 and P.L. 101-476, that are used to determine funding.

Because the syndromes are quantified, their applications to taxonic purposes can be adapted to the needs of the specific situation. The explicit demarcation of a normal range (T scores <67), borderline clinical range (T scores 67-70), and clinical range (T scores >70) offers three categories that are based directly on the distributions of scores obtained by normative and clinical samples on all eight syndromes, as rated by all three types of informants. If dichotomous classification as normal versus deviant is preferred, the borderline range can be combined with the clinical range. This has been found to yield better discrimination between referred and nonreferred samples than does combining the borderline range with the normal range (Achenbach, 1991b, 1991c, 1991d).

Chapter 5 presents various ways of classifying children according to their scores on the syndromes, while Chapter 7 illustrates ways of using the syndromes for practical and research purposes. In all applications of the syndromes, users should remember that they provide standardized descriptions of children's problems as reported by particular informants. A child's standing on a syndrome, as reported by a particular informant, consists of the sum of scores on all the items of the syndrome. T scores based on the normative sample for the child's sex and age scored by the relevant type of informant indicate how the reported problems compare with those typically reported for the child's peers.

High scores on particular syndromes scored by particular informants should not necessarily be equated with particular disorders. Furthermore, high scores on multiple syndromes do not necessarily mean that a child has multiple disorders. Instead, high scores on multiple syndromes as reported by a particular informant or on different syndromes as reported by different informants may represent patterns that reflect a child's functioning in a more differentiated way than does classification according to deviance on individual syndromes or according to individual diagnostic categories. For example, a child who is deviant on the Withdrawn, Anxious/ Depressed, and Aggressive Behavior syndromes may have an overall pattern of angry alienation rather than three separate disorders. To identify patterns of syndrome scores that can form a multisyndrome basis for taxonomy, we have performed cluster analyses on large samples of CBCL, TRF, and YSR profiles, as described in Chapter 4.

SUMMARY

This chapter presented the derivation of cross-informant syndrome constructs from the CBCL, TRF, and YSR. Separate principal components/varimax analyses were performed on clinical samples of each sex, within particular age ranges, scored on the CBCL, TRF, or YSR. For each instrument, *core syndromes* were constructed from the problem items that were found to co-occur for a majority of the sex/age groups that were analyzed separately on that instrument. The core syndromes from the three instruments were then compared to identify problem items that were present in the corresponding core syndromes for at least two of the three instruments. These items were used to define eight *cross-informant syndrome constructs* that can be scored from all three instruments.

The scales for scoring the syndromes are normed separately for each sex in particular age ranges, as rated by each type of informant. In addition to the items that define the cross-informant syndrome constructs, the instrument-specific versions of some syndrome scales include a few items that were strongly associated with the core syndrome derived only from that instrument. The syndrome scales and profiles on which the scales are scored provide standardized ways to describe children's problems as seen by different informants. The norms for the scales enable users to compare what those informants report for a particular child with what similar informants report for large normative samples of children.

Chapter 4
Empirically Based Profile Types

The syndromes described in Chapter 3 reflect sets of problems that co-occur. However, the syndromes do not necessarily represent groups of children who share similar overall patterns of problems. Although it is possible that a particular syndrome represents a group of children who are deviant only on that syndrome, numerous studies have shown that many children who are deviant in one area are also deviant in other areas as well. When deviance is assessed in terms of diagnoses, the finding that individuals qualify for multiple diagnoses is called *comorbidity* (e.g., Steingard, Biederman, Doyle, & Sprich-Buckminster, 1992; Walker et al., 1991). Comorbidity refers to the co-existence of different disorders in the same individual.

When particular combinations of diagnoses occur at greater than chance rates, it is often inferred that there must be a systematic relation between the different disorders represented by the diagnoses. However, apparent comorbidity may also reflect mismatches between diagnostic categories and the actual patterning of disorders. For example, comorbidity rates of 84 to 96% have been found between DSM diagnoses of Oppositional Defiant Disorder and Conduct Disorder (Faraone, Biederman, Keenan, & Tsuang, 1991; Spitzer, Davies, & Barkley, 1990; Walker et al., 1991). Rather than reflecting the co-occurrence of two different disorders, such high rates of comorbidity suggest that the diagnostic categories do not validly distinguish between different disorders (Achenbach, 1993a).

Until the boundaries between diagnostic categories for childhood disorders are better validated and more reliably applied, findings that children qualify for multiple diagnoses should not necessarily be construed as indicating the systematic co-occurrence of different disorders. Instead, such findings invite closer scrutiny of the co-occurring problems to identify patterns that may provide a better basis for taxonomy than the existing diagnostic categories do.

Not only the co-occurrence of categorical diagnoses, but also correlations between quantitatively scored syndromes have shown that children reported to be deviant in one area tend to be deviant in other areas as well. For example, positive correlations have been found among all syndrome scales of the CBCL, TRF, and YSR for both referred and nonreferred samples (Achenbach, 1991b, 1991c, 1991d). This pattern of positive correlations among problem scales is analogous to the pattern of positive correlations typically found among tests of different aspects of cognitive ability, such as the subtests of the Wechsler (1991) intelligence scales.

There are many possible reasons for the correlations among syndrome scales. One possible reason is that risks for particular kinds of problems are likely to be correlated with risks for other kinds of problems. Another possible reason is that high scores at early ages on one syndrome, such as Attention Problems, may be followed by high scores at later ages on another syndrome, such as Delinquent Behavior, as has been shown in longitudinal research (Stanger, Mc-Conaughy, & Achenbach, 1992).

Because we do not assume that each syndrome necessarily represents a categorically separate disorder, the positive correlations among them are viewed simply as quantitative descriptions of the degree to which the scores on one scale tend to covary with the scores on other scales.

As reported in Chapter 3, second-order factor analyses of correlations among the syndromes have yielded groupings that we have designated as Internalizing and Externalizing. Children can be classified as manifesting primarily Internalizing problems, primarily Externalizing problems, or a mixture of both. However, the Internalizing versus

Externalizing distinction is quite global. To determine whether we could identify more differentiated profile patterns that were shared by significant numbers of children, we performed cluster analyses of profiles of scores on the eight cross-informant syndromes. Like the derivation of the eight syndromes themselves, the derivation of profile patterns started with separate analyses of each sex within the age ranges that were used to norm the syndromes scored from the CBCL, TRF, and YSR. We compared the results for the various sex/age groups to identify *core profile patterns* for each instrument. We then computed correlations between the core profile patterns from the three instruments to identify *cross-informant profile patterns*. This chapter reports our cluster analytic procedures and findings.

CLUSTER ANALYSES OF PROFILES

There are many approaches to cluster analysis (Romesburg, 1984, provides extensive illustrations). The approach that is most relevant to constructing taxonomies of profile patterns starts with a sample of subjects, each of whom has scores on the same set of variables. For our purposes, subjects' scores on the eight cross-informant syndromes were the input for cluster analysis. Each subject's profile pattern was operationally defined by that subject's scores on the eight syndromes. The goal was to identify groups of subjects whose patterns of scores were similar.

Measuring Similarity Between Profiles

Based on comparisons of different methods of measuring similarity between profiles, the *intraclass correlations* (ICCs) between profiles appeared to be especially appropriate (Edelbrock & McLaughlin, 1980). Like Pearson *r*, the ICC represents the similarity between two sets of scores in terms of numbers ranging from -1.00 (perfect negative relation between two sets of scores) to +1.00 (perfect positive relation between two sets of scores). The size of Pearson r is governed mainly by the similarity between the rankings of corresponding scores from the two sets. When computed between two profiles of scores, such as the eight syndrome scores of Subject 1 versus the eight syndrome scores of Subject 2, Pearson r reflects the degree to which Subject 1's scores on syndromes I-VIII are in the same rank order as Subject 2's scores on syndromes I-VIII. (When applied to sets of scores from two subjects or on the same subject rated by two informants, the formula for Pearson r is said to yield a Q correlation. Q correlation refers to scores on multiple variables drawn from just two sources, in contrast to R correlation, which refers to scores on two variables drawn from multiple sources.)

As an example, suppose that Subject 1's highest score was on syndrome I, second highest was on syndrome II, and so on in descending order to syndrome VIII, which had the lowest score. Suppose, also, that Subject 2's scores followed exactly the same rank order as Subject 1's scores, with syndrome I having the highest score and syndrome VIII having the lowest score. The Pearson r (or Q correlation) between these two profiles of similarly ranked scores would be +1.00. Furthermore, the correlation would be +1.00 even if each of Subject 1's scores was much lower or higher than the corresponding score obtained by Subject 2. Pearson r would thus accurately reflect the fact that Subject 1's profile had the same *shape* as Subject 2's profile. However, Pearson r would not reflect the fact that Subject 1's scores were lower or higher than Subject 2's scores.

For some purposes, it may be useful to group subjects solely according to their profile shapes, without regard to differences in the elevation of their scores. However, if we wish to identify subjects who are similar with respect to both the elevation of their scores and the *shape* of their profiles, a measure of similarity that ignores the elevation would be less desirable than one that is affected by the elevation as well as by the shape of the profiles. In previous cluster analyses of syndrome scores, ICCs computed from one-way analyses of variance have yielded groups of subjects that are quite homogeneous with respect to both the elevation and shapes of their profiles (Edelbrock & McLaughlin, 1980). We therefore chose the ICC as our measure of similarity between profiles.

Centroid Cluster Analysis

From among the many clustering algorithms, we chose *centroid* analysis for its good performance when the number of scales was relatively small (e.g., eight syndromes) but the number of possible scores on each scale was relatively large (Edelbrock, 1979; Edelbrock & Achenbach, 1980). In centroid analysis, the clustering program first identifies the two subjects in a sample whose profiles are the most similar to each other. Because we used the ICC to measure the similarity between profiles, the two most similar subjects were those whose profiles had the highest ICCs with each other. In the analysis illustrated in Figure 4-1, Subjects 6 and 7 were found to be the most similar.

After the program found that Subjects 6 and 7 were the most similar, it created a miniature cluster consisting of these two subjects, which we will call cluster 6-7. The program then computed the *centroid* of their two profiles. The *centroid* is simply the profile formed by averaging the scores of two or more profiles. In this case, the mean of the scores obtained by Subjects 6 and 7 on syndrome I, the mean of their scores on syndrome II, etc., formed the centroid of Cluster 6-7. This centroid was a profile that was halfway between the profiles of Subjects 6 and 7. By representing what is similar about the cluster's members, the centroid of a cluster serves as the operational definition of the profile type represented by the cluster. Figure 4-2 illustrates the formation of a centroid by averaging the scale scores of two profiles.

After the first cluster consisting of two subjects has been formed, the program determines whether any subject remaining in the sample has a profile that is more similar to the centroid of the first cluster than to the profile of any remaining subject. This is done by computing ICCs between the centroids and the profiles of all subjects not already included in the first cluster. In Figure 4-1, this means that

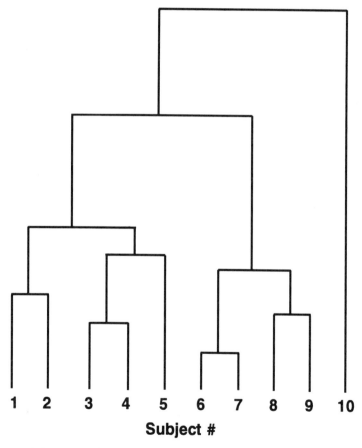

Figure 4-1. Illustration of a hierarchical clustering sequence. Clustering starts with a sample of subjects (#1-10) who each have a profile. Profiles having the highest ICCs with each other are then combined into clusters whose centroids are computed. Clusters whose ICCs are correlated highly with each other are combined into larger clusters.

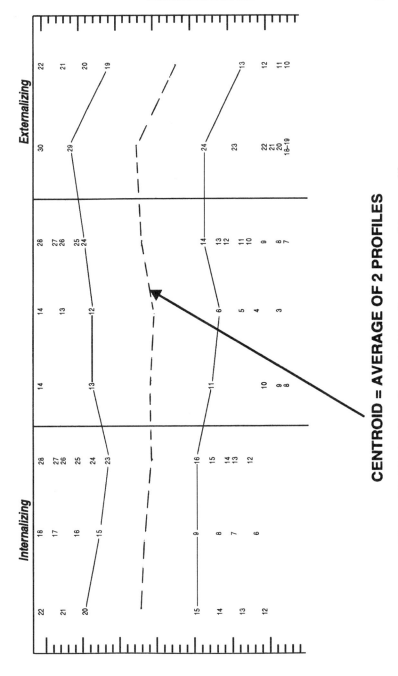

CENTROID = AVERAGE OF 2 PROFILES

Figure 4-2. Illustration of a centroid as the average of two profiles.

the program computed ICCs between the centroid of Cluster 6-7 and the individual profiles of Subjects 1, 2, 3, 4, 5, 8, 9, and 10. If the program found that a subject had a higher ICC with the centroid of Cluster 6-7 than with the profile of any unclustered subject (i.e., any subject other than 6 or 7), then this subject would be added to Cluster 6-7. Each time a new subject is added to a cluster, the centroid is recomputed as the mean of the group that now includes the new subject. Because the centroid is computed by averaging the scores of all members of the cluster, each member's contribution to the centroid has the same weight as every other member's contribution.

As shown in Figure 4-1, the program did not find any subject whose profile correlated more highly with the centroid of Cluster 6-7 than with the profile of an unclustered subject. Instead, the program found that the ICC between Subjects 3 and 4 was higher than the ICC of any unclustered subject with the centroid of Cluster 6-7 or of any other combination of unclustered subjects. The program therefore computed the centroid of the profiles for Subjects 3 and 4 to represent what was now Cluster 3-4.

In the next step, the program computed ICCs between the centroids of Clusters 3-4 and 6-7, as well as computing ICCs of the unclustered subjects with the centroids and with each other. Whenever the centroids of two clusters correlated more highly with each other than any unclustered profile correlated with another profile or a centroid, the two clusters were combined to form a new cluster. In Figure 4-1, for example, Clusters 6-7 and 8-9 became joined. When this happened, a new centroid was computed by averaging the profiles of all members of both clusters. The clustering program continued in a hierarchical fashion until all subjects became members of a single cluster. This single cluster is totally useless, because it is simply an undifferentiated collection of subjects identical to the unclustered sample with which the clustering procedure started. Clusters at intermediate levels in the hierarchy are likely to be the most useful, because they include more subjects than those near the bottom of the hierarchy, but are more homogeneous (i.e., their constituent members are more similar to each other) than clusters near the top of the hierarchy.

Use of Clinical Samples

The goal of our cluster analyses was to identify profile patterns that would discriminate among children whose problems differ descriptively and for whom differences may also be found in etiology, response to treatment, course, outcome, and other correlates. Because our focus was primarily on disorders, we performed our cluster analyses on children considered to be deviant enough to be referred for mental health or special education services. Our clinical cases were drawn from the samples used to derive the syndrome scales, as described by Achenbach (1991b, 1991c, 1991d). These included 4,455 CBCLs obtained from 52 mental health settings, 2,815 TRFs from 58 mental health and special education settings, and 1,272 YSRs from 26 mental health settings. Additional cases that had been obtained since the derivation of the syndromes were included to augment the samples.

Subjects of each sex were divided into the following age groups for analysis: CBCL ages 4-11 and 12-18; TRF ages 5-11 and 12-18; YSR ages 11-18. From each sex/age group scored on each instrument, two random samples (designated as A and B) were drawn from subjects who had total problem scores ≥30. This cutpoint of 30 was used to exclude subjects whose scores were too low to provide meaningful differentiation of profile patterns.

Standardization of Scores

Because the syndrome scales have different numbers of items, different mean scores, and different variances, profiles may have consistently lower scores on some scales and

higher scores on others. The tendency for most profiles to
be lower on certain scales and higher on others can cause
built-in patterning that will affect the clustering process. To
prevent built-in patterning from affecting our cluster
analyses, we converted the scores on each syndrome scale
to T scores having a mean of 50 and standard deviation of
10 within the A and B clinical samples for each sex/age
group on each instrument. (Note that these were *not
normalized T* scores based on percentiles of normative
samples like those used to assign T scores on the CBCL,
TRF, and YSR scoring profiles. Instead, these T scores were
computed by assigning 50 to the mean of the raw scores
obtained by a clinical sample and using 10 as the standard
deviation. If a distribution is perfectly normal, normalized
T scores based on percentiles and T scores based on
assignment of 50 to the mean and 10 to the standard
deviation yield the same results. In assigning T scores to the
clinical samples that were cluster analyzed, however, no
effort was made to normalize them by using percentiles.)

Cross-Validation of Profile Types

Cluster analysis groups together individuals who have
similar profile patterns within a particular sample. To
determine whether the profile types obtained in one sample
would replicate in another sample, we performed separate
cluster analyses of the A and B clinical samples for each
sex/age group on each instrument.

A centroid from sample A was considered to be cross-
validated if it obtained a significant ($p \leq .05$) ICC with a
centroid from Sample B, and vice versa. When such
centroids were found, the Sample A version was averaged
with the Sample B version to form a new centroid that was
retained for that sex/age group scored on the instrument in
question, i.e., the CBCL, TRF, or YSR. The A and B
samples each numbered 280 subjects, except for the 12-18-

year-old girls on the TRF, where the available referred subjects who scored ≥30 limited the samples to 231 and 232.

Derivation of Core Profile Types for Each Instrument

For the CBCL, separate cluster analyses were performed on the A and B samples of 4- to 11- and 12- to 18-year-olds of each sex. The input to the cluster analyses consisted of the unclustered profiles of all the individual subjects in a sample. Following a hierarchical sequence like the one illustrated in Figure 4-1, the individual profiles were combined into ever larger clusters until they were all placed in a single cluster. For every analysis, the hierarchical levels were examined to identify points at which most subjects were included in clusters of ≥8 subjects. (To ensure that clusters reflected similarities among a sufficient number of subjects, we retained only those that included ≥8 subjects.) Levels were selected where the centroids of the clusters displayed patterns that distinguished them from other centroids and where the centroids preserved their form in the succeeding levels of the hierarchy.

The 16-cluster to 20-cluster levels generally produced well-differentiated clusters that included ≥8 subjects and that survived well in succeeding steps. Across the different sex/age groups on the different instruments, the 18-cluster level was selected as a good representative of the findings. We therefore computed the ICCs between the centroids of the 18-cluster level from each A and B sample. Because only clusters that included ≥8 subjects were retained, fewer than 18 centroids were actually intercorrelated from each A and B sample.

From each pair of centroids found to correlate significantly ($p \leq .05$) from the A and B clusters, the A and B centroids were averaged to produce a centroid that would be used to characterize one profile type derived from one sex/age group on the CBCL. Because the A and B clusters usually included different numbers of subjects, the centroid from the A version of a cluster was weighted by the number of subjects in the A version. Similarly, the centroid from the B version of the cluster was weighted by the number of subjects in the B version. To identify core profile types that characterized a majority of the sex/age groups on the CBCL, we then computed ICCs between the centroids retained from each sex/age group and the centroids retained from each of the other sex/age groups. Those centroids that correlated significantly with centroids from at least 3 of the 4 sex/age groups were averaged with their counterparts to represent the *core profile types* for the CBCL.

The same procedure was followed for the TRF and YSR. For each of the four sex/age groups scored on the TRF, we first identified centroids from the A and B samples that correlated significantly with each other. We then identified those centroids that significantly correlated with counterparts in at least 3 of the 4 sex/age groups. The centroids that correlated significantly with each other were then averaged to represent the core profile types for the TRF. Because there were only two sex/age groups for the YSR (boys and girls aged 11-18), centroids from both groups had to correlate significantly with each other to be retained as a core profile type for the YSR.

Cross-Informant Profile Types

To identify profile patterns that were similar across the three instruments, we next computed ICCs between the core profile centroids from the CBCL, TRF, and YSR with each other. If the centroids from at least 2 of the 3 instruments correlated significantly, we considered them to represent *cross-informant profile types*. These types represented patterns that were shared by groups of children of both sexes, and different ages, rated by different informants. If a core profile centroid from one instrument did not correlate significantly with a centroid from another instrument, it was retained as a core profile type for classifying subjects only on the instrument from which it was derived. Figure 4-3 summarizes the steps in deriving core profile types and cross-informant profile types.

RESULTS OF THE CLUSTER ANALYSES

The ICCs among core profile centroids from the three instruments yielded four profile types meeting our criterion of significant ICCs among centroids from ≥ 2 instruments.

To avoid obscuring the effects of the instrument-specific items on the syndrome scales and the different distributions of scores obtained from different informants, we did not average the core profile types from each instrument into centroids representing the cross-informant profile types. Instead, we retained the core profile types from each instrument as a basis for classifying individual children. Nevertheless, the cross-informant profile types that represent significantly intercorrelated core types can be described in terms of the syndromes on which they tended to have their highest scores. The four patterns that qualified as cross-informant profile types are designated as follows: *Withdrawn, Somatic Complaints, Social Problems,* and *Delinquent-Aggressive.* For three of the cross-informant profile types, all combinations of core types from the CBCL, TRF, and YSR correlated significantly ($p < .05$) with each other. For the fourth type (designated as *Social Problems*), the YSR core type correlated significantly with the TRF and CBCL types, but the ICC of .54 between the CBCL and TRF core types reached only $p = .06$.

Low, intermediate, and high syndrome scores all contributed to determining which subjects were grouped together in the cluster analyses, which centroids from each sex/age group correlated significantly with centroids from other sex/age groups, and which core profile types from each instrument correlated significantly with those from other instruments. As a result, the core profile types that were considered to collectively indicate a cross-informant profile

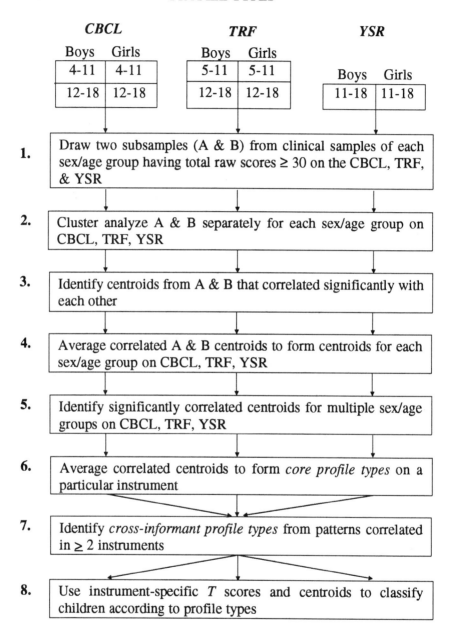

Figure 4-3. Summary of steps in developing profile types that are common to the CBCL, TRF, and YSR profiles.

type did not have exactly the same shapes. Even though three of the four cross-informant types are designated by the single scale having the highest peak, scores on the remaining seven scales are equally important in defining each type.

In addition to the four cross-informant types, the following qualified as core profile types or were retained for particular sex/age groups on the CBCL: *Social Problems-Attention Problems*, CBCL ages 12-18 only; *Withdrawn-Anxious/Depressed-Aggressive*, CBCL boys only; *Delinquent*, found in three of the four CBCL groups and employed as a core profile type for all four CBCL groups. On the TRF: *Attention Problems*, all four TRF groups; *Withdrawn-Thought Problems*, TRF ages 5-11. On the YSR, a profile type for both sexes that was high only on the Social Problems syndrome was designated as *YSR Social Problems* to distinguish it from the cross-informant Social Problems type; *Delinquent*, YSR girls only; *Attention Problems-Delinquent-Aggressive*, YSR boys only. Figures 4-4 through 4-6 display the core profile types and the types that were specific to particular sex/age groups on the CBCL, TRF, and YSR, respectively.

CORRELATING INDIVIDUAL PROFILES WITH PROFILE TYPES

The foregoing sections described the derivation of profile types via cluster analysis. The aim was to detect profile patterns that could be used to identify children who have similar patterns of scores on the eight cross-informant syndromes of the CBCL, TRF, and YSR. The 1993 editions of the computer programs for the CBCL, TRF, and YSR, as well as the cross-informant program, use the following procedure to compute ICCs between the syndrome scores obtained by individual children and the profile types shown in Figures 4-4 to 4-6. (Hand-computation of profile ICCs is too laborious to be practical.)

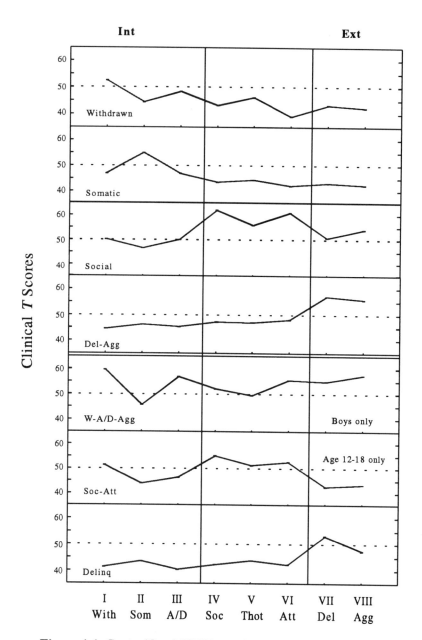

Figure 4-4. Centroids of CBCL versions of cross-informant profile types (above double line) and profile types specific to the CBCL (below double line).

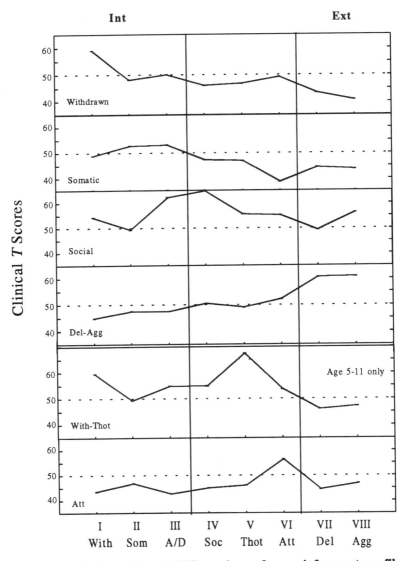

Figure 4-5. Centroids of TRF versions of cross-informant profile types (above double line) and profile types specific to the TRF (below double line.)

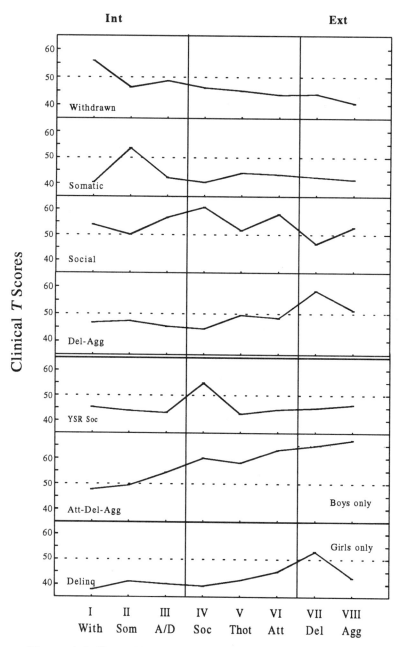

Figure 4-6. Centroids of YSR versions of cross-informant profile types (above double line) and profile types specific to the YSR (below double line).

1. Children with total problem scores <30 are excluded from the computation of ICCs because their scores are too low to afford sufficient differentiation of profile patterns.

2. A child's raw scores on the eight syndrome scales are converted to clinical T scores based on the combined A and B clinical samples for each sex/age group described earlier. Note that these clinical T scores are *not* the same as the T scores displayed to the right of the hand-scored and computer-scored profiles. The T scores displayed on the right side of the profiles are based on *nonreferred normative samples*, as detailed in the manuals for the CBCL, TRF, and YSR (Achenbach, 1991b, 1991c, 1991d). The T scores based on the normative samples indicate the degree to which a child's score on each syndrome scale of the CBCL, TRF, or YSR deviates from the normative sample of nonreferred peers scored on the same instrument. The T scores derived from the A and B clinical samples, by contrast, indicate the degree to which a child's syndrome scores deviate from those of *clinically referred* peers. Clinical samples were used to standardize scores because the profile types are intended to identify problem patterns among children who are apt to be candidates for professional help.

3. After a child's raw syndrome scores are converted to clinical T scores based on the relevant clinical sample, ICCs are computed between the child's T scores and the T scores that define the profile types from the CBCL (Figure 4-4), TRF (Figure 4-5), or YSR (Figure 4-6).

4. Along the bottom of the printout of the child's profile, the ICC is displayed between the child's

profile pattern and each of the profile types for that child's sex and age on the relevant instrument. The four cross-informant types are printed in capital letters on the left side. As an example, Figure 3-2 indicates that 15-year-old Ginny's CBCL profile had the following ICCs with the CBCL profile types for 12-18-year-old girls: *Withdrawn* ICC = -.581; *Somatic Complaints* ICC = -.367; *Social Problems* ICC = .585; *Delinquent-Aggressive* ICC = .266; *Social-Attention Problems* ICC = .279; *Delinquent* ICC = -.172. The ICCs are stored in the file of scored data created by the program. (Because the printed profile compares the child's syndrome scores to those of the *nonclinical normative* samples, the visible profile may not look like the profile type yielding the highest ICC.)

5. Any ICCs $\geq$.445 are marked with two asterisks to indicate that they are statistically significant at $p \leq$.05 by one-tailed test. (A one-tailed test is used because only positive ICCs are considered in the classification of children according to profile types.) Although .445 may seem like a relatively small correlation, an ICC is numerically lower than the more familiar Pearson r indicating the same degree of association. To depict relations between ICCs and Pearson rs for our profiles, Figure 4-7 shows the mean Pearson r obtained at various levels of ICC between CBCL profile types and the profiles of subjects included in the A and B samples of the four CBCL sex/age groups. Note that an ICC of .445 is approximately equivalent to a Pearson r of .59.

6. Users can classify children according to the profile types with which the children's profiles have the highest ICCs. Because the ICCs provide a quantitative measure of similarity to the profile types,

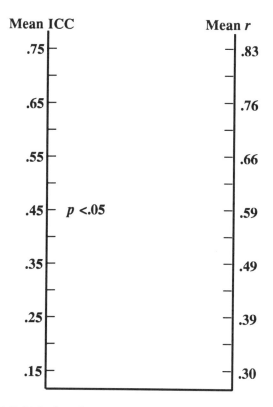

Figure 4-7. Relations between intraclass correlations (ICC) and Pearson correlations (*r*) computed between CBCLs and the core CBCL profile types. Each interval includes subjects whose ICCs ranged from .05 below the mean shown to .05 above the mean (e.g., the interval for mean ICC = .15 included subjects with ICCs from .10 to .20.)

classification need not be all-or-none. That is, users can decide how high the ICC should be to classify a child according to a particular profile type. The higher the ICC selected as the cutpoint, the more similar the group members will be to the profile type and to each other. However, the higher the cutpoint, the fewer the children who will qualify for each type. Because some children may have ICCs above the cutpoint with more than one type, users can decide

whether to assign the child to the type with which
the child's ICC is highest, or to apply other criteria
for classifying such cases. (Note that the ICCs *do not
indicate severity of problems. They merely indicate
the degree of resemblance to profile types.* However,
some types may involve greater severity than others.)

For quick reference, steps 1-6 are summarized in Table
4-1.

DISTRIBUTIONS OF PROFILE TYPES

To provide a picture of how the profile types are
distributed in diverse clinical samples, we computed the
ICCs of profiles scored for clinically referred children with
each of the profile types that was relevant for their sex, age,
and the instrument on which they were scored. The clinical
samples were those from which we drew the A and B
samples of each sex/age group in which to do the initial
cluster analyses. However, except for the 12-18-year-old girls
scored on the TRF, the total clinical sample for each group
was considerably larger than the two A and B subsamples,
which totalled 560 for each sex/age group on each
instrument.

Table 4-2 displays the N for the samples of each sex/age
group scored on each instrument, after excluding children
with total problem scores <30. The numbers in the body of
the table indicate the percent of each sample whose highest
significant ICC ($\geq$.445) was with each of the types relevant
to the particular sex/age group and instrument. For example,
to the right of the first cross-informant type (*Withdrawn*),
the 7 indicates that 7% of the CBCLs for 4-11-year-old boys
correlated highest with the cross-informant profile designated
as *Withdrawn*.

As shown in Table 4-2, the cross-informant Delinquent-
Aggressive type classified the largest percent of most groups
on the CBCL, TRF, and YSR. The percentages classified by

Table 4-1
Summary of Steps in Classifying Children
According to Profile Types

---

1. Exclude children with total problem raw scores <30.

2. Convert raw syndrome scores to T scores based on clinical samples.

3. Compute ICCs between child's T scores & T scores that define profile types for the relevant instrument.

4. Profile printout displays ICCs between the child's profile & relevant profile types.

5. ICCs $\geq$.445 are marked by two asterisks indicating $p \leq$.05 by one-tailed test.

6. Users can classify children according to highest ICC or other user-selected criteria.

---

this type ranged from 9 to 11% on the CBCL, from 14 to 16% on the TRF and from 8 to 10% on the YSR. For several groups, other profile types also involve elevations of the Externalizing syndromes. These include the Withdrawn-Anxious/Depressed-Aggressive type for boys and the Delinquent type for both sexes on the CBCL, as well as the Delinquent type for girls and the Attention Problems-Delinquent-Aggressive type for boys on the YSR. When children classified by these types are added to the children classified by the Delinquent-Aggressive types, 14 to 22% of the children in our clinical samples had profiles that were most similar to types showing high elevations on External-izing scales. However, some of these types either were elevated only on the Delinquent syndrome or were elevated

Table 4-2
Percentage of Each Clinical Sample Having ICC ≥.445 With Each Profile Type[a]

Profile Type	CBCL Boys 4-11	CBCL Boys 12-18	CBCL Girls 4-11	CBCL Girls 12-18	TRF Boys 5-11	TRF Boys 12-18	TRF Girls 5-11	TRF Girls 12-18	YSR Boys 11-18	YSR Girls 11-18
N =	1,392	1,266	790	646	1,241	813	610	463	860	670
Cross-Informant										
Withdrawn	7	7	7	6	11	13	14	16	7	10
Somatic Complaints	7	7	9	9	8	6	9	7	7	6
Social Probs.	8	7	8	5	6	7	4	7	7	7
Delinquent-Aggressive	10	9	9	11	16	16	15	14	10	8
CBCL Only										
Withdrawn-Anx./Dep.-Aggressive	3	5	NA	NA	NA	NA	NA	NA	NA	NA
Social Probs.-Attention Probs.	NA	7	NA	8	NA	NA	NA	NA	NA	NA
Delinquent	7	8	5	8	NA	NA	NA	NA	NA	NA

TRF Only										
Withdrawn-Thought Probs.	NA	NA	NA	NA	4	NA	6	NA	NA	NA
Attention Probs.	NA	NA	NA	NA	12	11	9	6	NA	NA
YSR Only										
YSR Social Probs.[b]	NA	NA	NA	NA	NA	NA	NA	NA	7	7
Attention Probs.-Delinquent	NA	NA	NA	NA	NA	NA	NA	NA	NA	NA
Aggressive	NA	NA	NA	NA	NA	NA	NA	NA	5	NA
Delinquent	NA	NA	NA	NA	NA	NA	NA	NA	NA	6
Percentage having ICCs from .001 to .444 with ≥1 type	49	43	53	46	39	42	39	45	50	47
Percentage having all ICCs ≤.000	8	8	9	8	5	5	3	5	8	10

Note. NA indicates groups for which particular profile types are not applicable.
[a]Subjects having total problem scores ≥30 and ICCs ≥.445 are classified according to the profile type with which they had their highest ICC.
[b]Social Problems type specific to YSR (differs from cross-informant Social Problems type).

on a combination of Externalizing syndromes with other syndromes. One of these combinations (for boys on the CBCL) included elevations on the Withdrawn and Anxious/ Depressed syndromes from the Internalizing grouping, as well as the Aggressive Behavior syndrome.

The profile type that classified the second largest percentage of children was the TRF version of the cross-informant Withdrawn type, which classified from 11 to 16% of the four sex/age groups. This type also classified 10% of the girls scored on the YSR and from 6 to 7% of the other groups. The TRF Attention Problems type classified a relatively large percentage of boys, i.e., 12% at ages 5-11 and 11% at ages 12-18, but fewer girls, i.e., 9% at ages 5-11 and 6% at ages 12-18.

Children Not Assigned to Profile Types

The second to last row of Table 4-2 indicates the percentage of children whose profiles had positive ICCs that did not reach .445 with any type. The last row indicates the percentage who showed no similarity to any type (all their ICCs were ≤.000). For some purposes, users may wish to classify children according to profile types with which their ICCs are <.445. For example, an ICC of ≥.350 might be chosen as a cutpoint that would increase the number of children classified by types while still maintaining moderate similarity among those classified. The choice of .445 as a cutpoint is based on $p = .05$ as the conventional level of statistical significance. However, the ICCs represent continuous gradations of similarity to the centroids. Thus, an ICC of .350 indicates some similarity to a centroid even though it does happen to reach the $p = .05$ level of significance.

The children who did not correlate ≥.445 with any of the profile types include some who have idiosyncratic combinations of peaks, valleys, and overall elevations on the syndromes, as scored by a particular informant at a particular point in time. Some of these children may obtain profile patterns that would correlate ≥.445 with the identified types at another point in time or when scored by a different informant. It is also possible that their profiles would correlate ≥.445 with the centroids of groups that were too small to meet our criteria for retention as a profile type.

The fact that some children failed to correlate ≥.445 with an identified type does not mean either that their profiles are uninformative or that they do not have enough problems to need help. (Remember that the ICCs indicate *resemblance* to the profile types, rather than *severity of problems.*) The aim of scoring children on profiles is to capture the patterns of problems that are specific to each child, whether or not other children also share similar patterns. The primary data consist of ratings on specific problem items. These reflect what particular informants report about the child at a particular point in time.

The empirically derived syndromes aggregate the co-occurring problem items, thereby "chunking" the individual problem scores into scales. These syndrome scales facilitate cognitive processing of the overall picture presented by a particular informant's ratings of the problem items. Because the eight cross-informant scales are parallel on the profiles scored from parent-, teacher-, and self-reports, they also facilitate comparisons among the pictures presented by these three types of informants. The norms for the syndrome scales provide metrics for judging the degree of deviance indicated by the sum of a child's problem scores on each syndrome scale. In addition to aiding users in the assessment of individual children, the syndrome scales also provide foci for research on differences in the etiology, course, responsiveness to intervention, outcome, and other correlates of particular sets of problems.

Just as the syndrome scales reflect empirically derived aggregations of problem items, the profile types reflect empirically derived *patterns* of syndrome scores. Children whose patterns of syndrome scores resemble one profile type can be compared to children whose patterns resemble other profile types in order to test for differences in correlates.

Although all children obtain scores on each syndrome, computation of ICCs with profile types is restricted to total problem raw scores ≥30 in order to exclude children for whom differences between syndrome scores are likely to be based on too few items to be meaningful. The exclusion of these children, plus those who do not have significant ICCs with any profile type, is analogous to the exclusion of some problem items from the syndrome scales. The problems that are not on the syndrome scales were either too rare in clinical samples for inclusion in our analyses or did not meet our criteria for membership in the syndromes because they did not load highly enough on rotated principal components for enough sex/age groups.

The fact that some items are not on syndrome scales does not mean that they are unimportant. Each item may be quite important in its own right. By the same token, profile patterns that do not correlate significantly with a profile type are nevertheless important in evaluating the individual children who display them. Furthermore, it has been found that better results are obtained from cluster analyses that are allowed to exclude unusual profiles than from those that are forced to construct clusters including all profiles in a sample (Edelbrock, 1979).

SUMMARY

When deviance is defined in terms of DSM diagnoses, many children are found to meet criteria for multiple diagnoses. Termed *comorbidity*, this reflects the fact that children who have many problems of one kind tend to be deviant with respect to other kinds of problems as well. The tendency for multiple kinds of problems to co-occur is also reflected in the positive correlations among scores on empirically based syndromes.

To identify groups of children who have similar patterns of syndrome scores, we performed cluster analyses of the profiles of clinically referred children. To avoid built-in patterns that would arise from differences in the scale score distributions, scores on each syndrome scale were converted to clinical T scores for referred children in each sex/age group.

Intraclass correlations (ICCs) were used to measure the similarity between profiles. *Centroid cluster analysis* was then applied to the ICCs in order to identify clusters of children whose profiles were similar. A *centroid* is the profile formed by averaging the profiles of the members of a cluster. Clusters were retained if their centroids correlated significantly with a counterpart in a second clinical sample. The correlated centroids from the two clinical samples were averaged to form a new centroid representing the two samples combined.

Centroids that were significantly correlated among multiple sex/age groups scored on the CBCL, TRF, or YSR were averaged to form *core profile types* for the respective instruments. To identify *cross-informant profile types* that were similar across instruments, we computed ICCs between the core profile types from each instrument. The four profiles that met our criteria for cross-informant profile types were designated as: *Withdrawn, Somatic Complaints, Social Problems*, and *Delinquent-Aggressive*. Additional profile types retained for a single instrument were: CBCL—*Social Problems-Attention Problems, Withdrawn-Anxious/Depressed-Aggressive*, and *Delinquent*; TRF—*Attention Problems* and *Withdrawn-Thought Problems*; YSR—*YSR-Social Problems* and *Attention Problems-Delinquent-Aggressive*.

To measure the similarity between a child's profile and each of the types for the child's sex, age, and the relevant instrument, the 1993 IBM-compatible editions of the CBCL, TRF, YSR, and cross-informant programs compute the ICCs between the child's profile and each profile type. Because the printed profile compares the child's syndrome scores to those of the *nonclinical normative* samples, the visible profile type may not look like the profile type yielding the highest ICC. Table 4-2 displays the percentage of children whose highest significant ICC ($\geq.445$) was with each type. Children grouped according to these types can be compared on other variables to identify significant correlates of the types. Cutpoints lower than ICC .445 can be used to classify larger proportions of children but with lower degrees of similarity.

Chapter 5
Relations Between Taxonomies Based on Syndromes and Profiles

Chapter 3 described the derivation of syndromes from the problem items of the CBCL, TRF, and YSR. Chapter 4 described the derivation of profile types from the eight cross-informant syndromes that are common to the CBCL, TRF, and YSR. Each syndrome by itself and the patterns of syndrome scores embodied in the profile types offer ways to group children according to the kinds of problems reported for them. This chapter highlights the relations between taxonomies based on syndromes and profile types.

To illustrate relations between the syndromes and profile types, Figure 5-1 depicts the four cross-informant profile types in relation to the eight cross-informant syndromes. A line connects each cross-informant profile type to the syndrome(s) having the highest peak on the centroid of the profile type.

As was previously shown in Figures 4-4 to 4-6, the centroids of the profile types designated by a single peak are not uniformly low on all other syndromes. Recall that centroids are defined by clinical T scores. Thus, a T score of 50 for a centroid reflects the mean of the scores obtained by clinically referred children on a syndrome. The mean of raw scores obtained by clinically referred children is higher than the mean that would be obtained by nonreferred children. Accordingly, the syndrome scores that are $T < 50$ on a centroid do not indicate that children must have below-average scores on these syndromes to correlate significantly with the profile type. On the contrary, many raw scores that

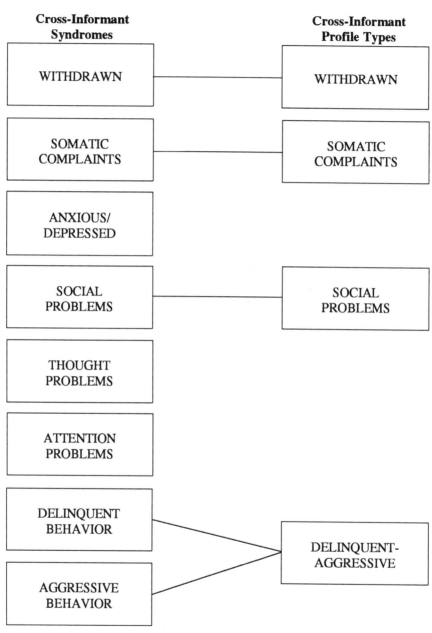

Figure 5-1. Relations between cross-informant syndromes and cross-informant profile types designated by the syndrome(s) having the highest peak(s) on each type.

are below average for the clinical samples from which the centroids were derived would be above average in normative samples of nonreferred children.

Figures 5-2 to 5-4 depict relations between the eight syndromes and the profile types that are specific to the CBCL, TRF, and YSR, respectively. As indicated in the figures, some types are limited to particular sex/age groups on a particular instrument.

Note that there is no single "correct" taxonomy. Instead, the same phenomena can be grouped in different ways for different purposes. A particular user may choose one taxonomic approach for one purpose and other taxonomic approaches for other purposes. Syndromes can be used taxonically in a variety of ways, as can profiles. Although taxonomies are intended to group phenomena according to the actual properties of the phenomena themselves, the particular properties that are chosen and the reliability and validity with which they are assessed may vary with the user's goals, the stage of knowledge, and the sophistication of the assessment procedures. Furthermore, some useful taxonic groupings may be based on transitory, state-like features. Other useful groupings may be based on more enduring, trait-like features. Rather than seeking a single pre-eminent taxonomy, users should therefore compare findings obtained from multiple approaches whenever possible.

SYNDROME-BASED TAXONOMIES

Each empirically based syndrome represents a set of co-occurring problems, rather than a "type" of child. Each child obtains a score on every syndrome scale, which is the sum of 0-1-2 scores on the items comprising the scale. The magnitude of the child's syndrome score reflects the degree to which particular kinds of problems are reported to be present.

As discussed in Chapter 2, the set of items comprising an empirically derived syndrome can be viewed as a

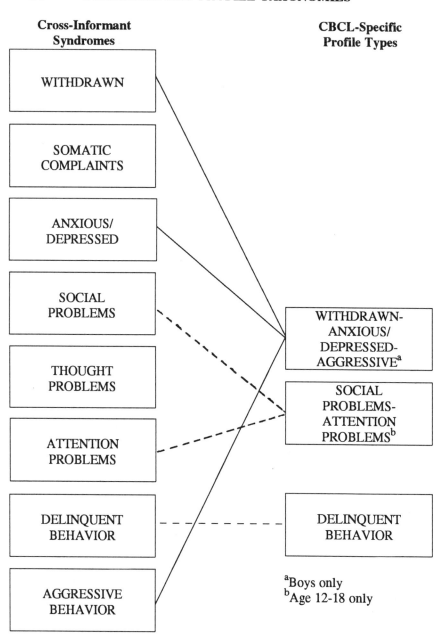

Figure 5-2. Relations between cross-informant syndromes and CBCL-specific profile types designated by the syndrome(s) having the highest peak(s) on each type.

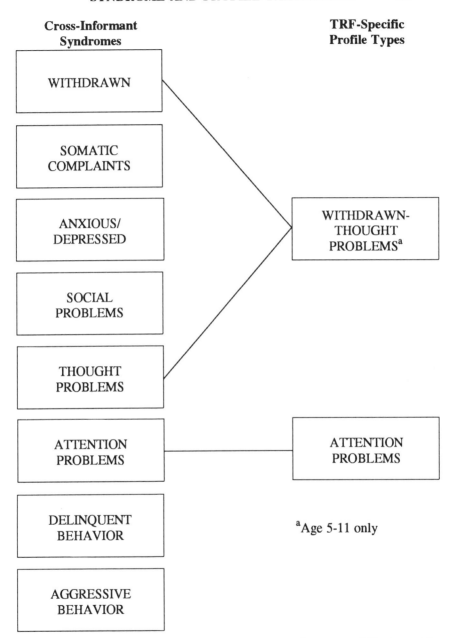

Figure 5-3. Relations between cross-informant syndromes and TRF-specific profile types designated by the syndrome(s) having the highest peak(s) on each type.

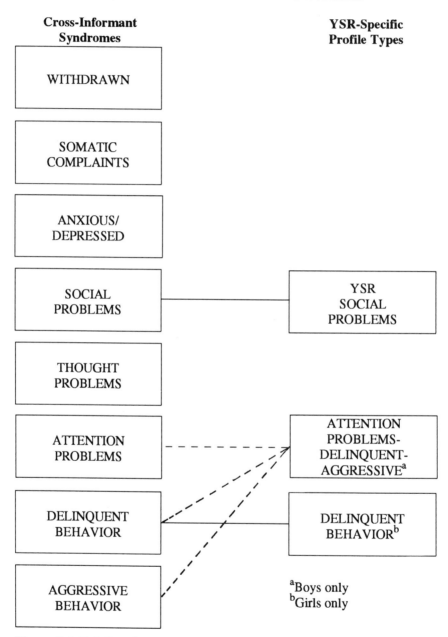

Figure 5-4. Relations between cross-informant syndromes and YSR-specific profile types designated by the syndrome(s) having the highest peak(s) on each type.

prototype—that is, a category defined by a set of imperfectly correlated features (Smith & Medin, 1981). The category represented by a syndrome is not assumed to encompass a totally homogeneous set of individuals. Instead, it represents a category of *problems* defined by their tendency to covary, as shown by principal components-varimax analyses of the correlations among them.

Children who have deviant scores on a particular syndrome can be viewed as a class. The members of this class share the distinction of having more problems of the type represented by the syndrome than do normative samples of their peers. The similarities reflected in a deviant score on a particular syndrome may provide important markers to guide the search for common etiological factors, accurate prognoses, and effective interventions. Such markers also make it possible to identify new cases that are similar to previous cases about which knowledge has been accumulated. Syndromes can thus alert us to other shared features that can be very useful. The following section outlines several procedures for grouping children according to their syndrome scores.

Single Sources of Syndrome Data

Taxonomy of child psychopathology involves many kinds of data. We will first discuss procedures for using syndromes based on only one source of data and then procedures that combine multiple sources.

Dichotomous Classification. The simplest approach to using a single source of data is to classify children as deviant on a syndrome if their score on that syndrome is above a particular cutpoint and nondeviant if their score is below the cutpoint. For example, if we wish to classify children as deviant versus nondeviant on the Aggressive Behavior syndrome, we might classify all those having T scores <67 as nondeviant and all those having T scores ≥ 67 as deviant.

In this example, the choice of $T = 67$ as the cutpoint was based on combining the borderline clinical range (T scores 67 to 70) with the clinical range (T scores >70). We have found that combining the borderline range with the clinical range discriminates better between referred and nonreferred samples than does combining the borderline range with the normal range (Achenbach 1991b, 1991c, 1991d).

If users wish to reduce the proportion of *false positives* (i.e., normal individuals who are incorrectly classified as deviant), they can combine the borderline range with the normal range. This raises the cutpoint to a higher T score, such as >70. However, raising the cutpoint increases the proportion of *false negatives* (truly deviant individuals who are incorrectly classified as normal).

Note that "truly deviant" implies the existence of some external gold standard that can tell us who really is deviant versus nondeviant. Such a gold standard is, however, merely a convenient fiction that facilitates reasoning about the consequences of using relatively low versus high cutpoints on distributions of problem scores. Because there is no gold standard for who "truly" does and does not have the disorder represented by the Aggressive Behavior syndrome, our judgments about particular cutpoints must be made in relation to other fallible criteria that can be applied to the same subjects.

The fact that there really is no infallible gold standard against which to test a particular taxonic procedure underlines the need for quantitative and probabilistic thinking in the development and applications of taxonomies, even when only dichotomous decisions are involved. Rather than expecting an infallible signal that a procedure accurately discriminates between those who truly do and do not have a particular disorder, we must continually try to increase the utility of multiple indices of the target variables.

Trichotomous Classification. In the preceding examples of dichotomous classification, the borderline range (T scores

67 to 70) was combined either with the normal range (T <67) or clinical range (T >70) to classify children as nondeviant versus deviant. This is warranted if users have overriding reasons for a dichotomous classification rather than a more differentiated classification. However, children scoring in the borderline range can be separated from those scoring in the normal and clinical ranges to form a trichotomous classification. The borderline range is demarcated on the distribution of syndrome scores to highlight the fact that neither the assessment procedures nor the disorders that they tap can actually divide all children into two groups who are intrinsically different from each other. Furthermore, both the psychometric discrimination between deviant and nondeviant groups and the underlying differences between these groups are fuzziest for children whose scores are closest to the cutpoints.

All scores may fluctuate somewhat from one assessment occasion to another. As a result, children whose scores are closest to the cutpoint are more likely to be misclassified on a particular occasion than are children whose scores are far above or below the cutpoint. This is true not only for quantitatively scored syndrome scales but also for categorical DSM diagnoses. Several studies have shown that many individuals who just meet or exceed the DSM lifetime criteria for a diagnosis (such as depression) on one occasion fail to meet the lifetime criteria on a subsequent occasion (Helzer, Spitznagel, & McEvoy, 1987; Robins, 1985; Vandiver & Sher, 1991; Wells, Burnham, Leake, & Robins, 1988). Thus, the tendency for people to report fewer symptoms in a second interview than in a first interview leads to a logical contradiction for categorical DSM diagnoses: As people's lifetimes lengthen, their cumulative record of disorders appears to decline.

It is seldom necessary or advisable to definitively classify all children as deviant versus nondeviant on the basis of any single criterion at a particular point in time. Incorrect or premature diagnostic classifications, for example, may stigmatize children without offering any compensating benefits. To take account of the greater difficulty of classifying children who are close to the cutpoint than those who are far above or below it, children who are close to the cutpoint can be withheld from groups classified as deviant versus nondeviant.

For some purposes, it may be advisable to reapply the same assessment procedure at a later date when the child's functioning may have moved more clearly into the deviant or nondeviant range. It is also desirable to apply additional assessment procedures that may collectively indicate whether some borderline cases are more appropriately classified as deviant or as nondeviant.

As a general rule, important decisions should not be based on only one source of data about children's problems. However, even when repeated and multiple assessment procedures are employed, some cases may not be clearly classifiable as deviant versus nondeviant with respect to a particular syndrome. In such cases, it may be better to allow them to remain classified as borderline rather than risking misclassifications that could do more harm than good.

Inclusion of the borderline range demarcated by T scores 67 to 70 on the empirically based syndromes has been found to produce better agreement between different informants than does dichotomous classification of children as deviant versus nondeviant (Achenbach, 1991a). Furthermore, when children scoring in the borderline range are excluded, the classification of the remaining children as deviant versus nondeviant discriminates more strongly between referred and nonreferred children than when borderline children are included (Achenbach, 1991b, 1991c, 1991d). Although the borderline range has been defined as T scores of 67 to 70 on the empirically based syndrome scales, other borderline ranges may be useful for particular purposes. Like the effects of particular dichotomous cutpoints, the effects of particular borderline ranges depend on the samples of scores to which they are applied and the use to which they are put.

Continuous Scores on a Single Syndrome. The inclusion of a borderline range takes advantage of more of the quantitative information provided by syndrome scale scores than does a dichotomous classification as deviant versus nondeviant. However, even the inclusion of the borderline range distinguishes among only three levels of scores on a continuous distribution comprised of many scores.

Although taxonomy is usually thought of in categorical terms, the features used to define behavioral/emotional disorders can seldom be reliably and validly assessed as present versus absent. Instead, distractibility, hyperactivity, sadness, somatic complaints, fighting, stealing, and other problems vary in degree. In addition, procedures for assessing such problems vary in the degree to which the target phenomena are detected and reported. Not only the assessment data but many of the underlying disorders to be assessed are also apt to vary in degree. For example, attention deficit disorders are not likely to exist solely in present versus absent form but to vary in severity.

Taxonic procedures designed to take account of quantitative variations in the phenomena to be classified are called *taxometric*. The term "taxometric" has been applied to the use of cluster analysis for classifying complex entities such as biological species (Sneath & Sokal, 1973). It has also been applied to the use of psychometric procedures for discriminating between schizotypes (people thought to have a genotype for schizophrenia) and nonschizotypes (Meehl & Golden, 1982).

Our use of principal components-varimax analysis to derive syndromes is taxometric in that it constructs groupings of problems from the quantitative relations among them. Furthermore, the sum of item scores on a syndrome is taxometric in the sense that it *measures* the degree to which a child is reported to manifest the problems of that syndrome.

If we think of each empirically based syndrome as measuring a particular set of co-occurring features, it makes sense to use the full range of possible scores on the syndrome to represent the degree to which a child manifests the problems comprising the syndrome. For analyses of relations to other variables, such as hypothesized etiological factors and outcome measures, the actual scores on each syndrome can be used. Use of the full range of continuous scores on the syndromes has been found to yield more accurate predictions of outcomes than did classification of children as deviant versus nondeviant on the same syndrome scales (McConaughy et al., 1992).

Continuous Scores on Multiple Syndromes. Because children obtain scores on multiple syndromes appropriate for their sex and age, the scores on multiple syndromes can be simultaneously included in analyses of relations to other variables, such as risk factors and outcome measures. For example, suppose we divide a sample of subjects into those found to have good outcomes and those found to have poor outcomes according to certain specific criteria. A discriminant analysis can then be done to construct the weighted combination of syndromes that most accurately classifies subjects into the good and poor outcome groups.

After cross-validation either in another sample or in a hold-out portion of the original sample, the weighted combination of syndromes can be used to identify other children most likely to have good outcomes versus those most likely to have poor outcomes. New interventions can then be developed to help those whose initial syndrome scores are similar to those initially manifested by the poor outcome group. Viewing syndrome scores from a measurement perspective thus opens up new ways to capitalize on the information that they convey.

Multiple Sources of Syndrome Data

The preceding sections dealt with the use of syndromes to make taxonic decisions based on a single source of data.

Because single sources seldom provide a comprehensive picture of children's functioning, it is important to consider ways in which multiple sources can contribute to taxonic decisions. The following sections present both categorical and taxometric approaches to using multiple sources of data in classifying children's problems according to syndromes.

Taxonomic Decision Tree. In using multisource data to classify children as deviant versus nondeviant on particular syndromes, one approach is to map out an explicit sequence of binary decisions involving all the relevant sources of data. The sequence of decisions can be visually represented in the form of a *taxonomic decision tree*, as illustrated in Figure 5-5.

The decision tree shows how data can be coordinated from multiple sources that each tap similar syndromes. The sources indicated at the top of the tree in Figure 5-5 include the CBCL, YSR, and TRF, plus instruments for scoring syndromes from clinical interviews (e.g., the *Semistructured Clinical Interview for Children*, "SCIC;" McConaughy & Achenbach, 1990) and direct observations in settings such as classrooms (e.g., the *Direct Observation Form*, "DOF;" see Achenbach, 1991b).

The SCIC and DOF do not yield scores on all the same syndromes as the CBCL, YSR, and TRF. However, the SCIC and DOF can be placed in the tree for making decisions about those syndromes that they do have in common with other instruments. Similarly, any other sources that distinguish between deviant and nondeviant scores on a common set of syndromes can be included at the top of the tree. Multiple informants of a particular type can also be listed as separate sources. For example, if a child's mother, father, and several teachers provide data, they can all be listed as separate sources at the top of the decision tree.

To illustrate use of the tree, suppose that we have data from multiple sources for an 11-year-old boy named Ben. The tree breaks the decision process into a series of steps

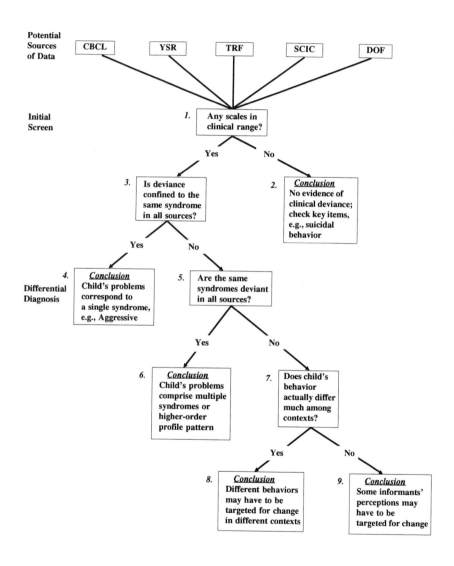

Figure 5-5. Decision tree for making taxonomic assignments from multiple sources of data.

marked by particular questions. As shown in *Box 1*, we first ask whether any syndromes from any source are in the clinical range. The possible answers are "yes" and "no." If the answer is "no," we move to *Box 2*, where the conclusion is drawn that Ben is not clinically deviant in terms of the syndrome scales scored from the available sources. However, this conclusion pertains only to the syndromes that were scored from the available sources of data. The data should still be examined for other indications of deviance, including specific problems that are of concern in their own right, such as suicidal behavior.

Returning now to *Box 1*, if the question about deviance on syndrome scales were answered "yes," we move to *Box 3*, which asks, "Is deviance confined to the same syndrome in all sources?" If this question is answered "yes," we move to *Box 4*, where the conclusion is drawn that the available sources point to deviance on a single syndrome, such as Aggressive Behavior.

On the other hand, if the question in *Box 3* were answered "no," we move to *Box 5*, where we ask whether the same combination of syndromes is deviant in all sources. If this question is answered "yes," we move to *Box 6*, where we conclude that Ben's problems are evident in multiple syndromes that are consistent across sources. The particular pattern of deviant syndromes may correspond to one of the profile types described in Chapter 4, or it may be specific to Ben or to particular groups of children or combinations of data not included in our empirically based profile types.

To return to *Box 5*, if the answer were "no," i.e., the same syndromes are not deviant in all sources, we move to *Box 7*. Here we ask whether Ben's behavior actually differs much among the contexts from which the data were obtained. To answer this question, we may need to obtain more data. For example, we could obtain direct observations in settings where they had not been obtained. Or we could interview the informants who had provided conflicting data in order to explore the reasons for the discrepancies. If the conclusion in *Box 8* is that Ben really does show different kinds of problems in different contexts, then different behaviors may have to be targeted for change in the different contexts. However, if the discrepancies between informants' reports are not borne out, then some of the informants might be appropriate targets for change, as concluded in *Box 9*.

The taxonomic decision tree can be used where conclusions about the particular areas of deviance are to be drawn from multisource data about an individual child such as Ben. It can also be used to subdivide groups of children according to the particular patterns of deviance they display and to determine the proportion who are not deviant on any syndrome, those who are deviant on only one syndrome (grouped according to the syndrome on which they are deviant), and those who share each of the other patterns.

Averaging Continuous Scores for Individuals. The taxonomic decision tree provides a strategy for coordinating dichotomous data (deviant versus nondeviant) from multiple sources regarding multiple syndromes. If it is not necessary to classify children as deviant versus nondeviant on each syndrome, continuous scores from multiple sources can be applied to taxonic tasks in several ways.

In assessing individual children, the T scores for a particular syndrome scored from multiple informants can be averaged to obtain a mean T score for the child. (T scores rather than raw scores should be averaged, because a particular T score indicates a similar degree of deviance on all scales; raw scores, by contrast, are affected by differences in the numbers and prevalence of problems on scales scored by different informants.) For example, if 11-year-old Ben had been rated by his mother and father on the CBCL, two teachers on the TRF, and himself on the YSR, his five T scores on each syndrome could be averaged to provide a multi-informant syndrome pattern. This would provide a summary picture of the areas in which his scores were consistently low and high across all informants. If the mean

T score for the Aggressive Behavior syndrome were 80 and the mean T score for the Somatic Complaints syndrome were 55, this would be good evidence for cross-situationally consistent deviance in aggression and evidence against any deviance in somatic complaints.

It is nevertheless important to examine the scores obtained from each informant. It may be found, for example, that the Attention Problems syndrome was scored in the clinical range by both teachers but in the normal range by both parents and Ben himself. The intermediate score obtained by averaging the five scores would thus obscure the big differences between the scores from different informants. The differences should be taken into account when evaluating Ben, as they reveal that his behavior is seen quite differently by his teachers than by his parents and himself. The cross-informant computer program for comparing CBCLs, TRFs, and the YSR provides item-by-item and scale-by-scale comparisons, plus Q correlations among informants. The specific agreements and disagreements between sources of data, as well as the degree of agreement, are thus highlighted (Achenbach, 1991a, provides illustrations).

Averaging Continuous Scores for Groups. When multisource data are available for a large sample of children, the raw scale scores within that sample can be converted to standard scores separately for each type of informant. (Note that this involves computing standard scores specific to the user's sample, rather than applying the T scores based on the national normative sample.) For example, if scores for the same subjects are available from their mothers, fathers, two teachers, and the subjects themselves, the distribution of the mothers' scores on the Aggressive Behavior syndrome can be converted to T scores with a mean of 50 and standard deviation of 10 for this particular sample. (If preferred, the raw scores can be converted to z scores with a mean of 0 and standard deviation of 1; T scores are more commonly used, because they avoid negative scale scores.) The same can be done for the fathers' scores, teachers' scores and self-report scores.

By converting to standard scores, the scores from the different kinds of informants for this sample of children are all given the same mean and variance. Averages computed from the standard scores obtained from the different informants will therefore not be affected by any tendency for the scores from informants in the sample to be distributed differently than those in the normative sample, on which T scores displayed on the profiles are based.

To compute each subject's multisource score on a syndrome such as Aggressive Behavior, the sample-based T scores (or z scores if preferred) are averaged across the five informants for that subject. In research that tests predictors, treatment outcomes, or correlates of a syndrome such as Aggressive Behavior, the aggregation of multisource data in this way is likely to provide more reliable and valid measures of each syndrome than if only a single source is used. Averaging standard scores across all available informants for each subject also has the advantage of retaining subjects who lack scores from some of the informants. However, because some sources may provide more reliable and valid data about certain syndromes than other sources do, it is also desirable to analyze the data from each source separately. Conclusions that are supported by analyses of each source separately and combined will inspire the most confidence.

Weighting Continuous Scores. In addition to the averaging of unweighted standard scores from multiple informants, multisource scores can be employed in multivariate analyses that selectively weight the scores from each source in order to maximize their collective association with other variables. For example, suppose that we wish to use CBCL, TRF, and YSR scores on the Aggressive Behavior syndrome as outcome measures to compare the effects of three different interventions for aggression. If we use multivariate analysis of variance (MANOVA) in which the CBCL, TRF, and YSR ratings are the dependent variables, MANOVA would optimally weight the three types of scores to detect outcome differences among the intervention groups.

Other approaches to weighting multi-informant ratings in relation to an external criterion include multiple regression and discriminant analyses. In these analyses, children are first scored or classified on a particular outcome variable. For example, in a long-term follow-up of clinical services, we might score children on a continuum from good to poor outcomes on a global measure of functioning. If we had obtained syndrome scores from multiple informants at intake into the clinical service, we could regress the outcome scores on the ratings from different informants to obtain an optimally weighted combination of intake scores for predicting outcomes. If we use the outcome measure to divide subjects into two groups, such as good versus poor outcomes, multiple discriminant analysis could be similarly used to weight the initial syndrome scores as predictors of the dichotomous outcomes. Before much confidence is invested in the weighting of predictors and the strength of the predictive relations, we should cross-validate the regression and discriminant analyses in other samples or in hold-out portions of the original sample (SAS Institute, 1990).

PROFILE-BASED TAXONOMIES

Children who are deviant on a particular syndrome may vary greatly with respect to their standing on other syndromes. Some may be deviant on no other syndromes, whereas others are deviant on any combination of other syndromes. Not only deviance versus nondeviance but the overall profile pattern of high, intermediate, and low scores across all syndromes may vary among children who are similar in being deviant on a particular syndrome. In fact, any combination of scores on other syndromes might be found among children who are deviant on a particular syndrome.

Research, training, and clinical services have tended to focus on deviance in one particular area as if it represented a homogeneous category of children. There are thus many references to "the depressed child," "the ADHD child," "conduct disordered children," etc. As a consequence, it is easy to slip into the habit of viewing children designated by one of these labels as a homogeneous group. Labels such as these may be hard to avoid, but they oversimplify the task of grouping cases according to all the features that could contribute to useful distinctions. This is especially true when we lack knowledge of specific etiologies that could serve as criteria for defining disorders. Rather than prematurely committing ourselves to particular criteria for disorders, we need to compare various ways of dividing up the phenotypic variations between children in order to identify features that may effectively distinguish between underlying differences.

As shown in previous sections, syndrome scores can be used in various ways to classify children according to their reported problems. The overall *pattern* of scores on the eight cross-informant syndromes can also be used for various taxonic purposes. Chapter 4 described the procedure for deriving profile types and for computing ICCs to measure the similarity between a child's profile pattern and the relevant profile types.

Unlike the syndromes, the profile types are not intended to distinguish between deviant and nondeviant children nor to directly indicate the degree of deviance. Instead, they are intended to distinguish among patterns of problems reported for children whose scores are high enough (i.e., total problems ≥ 30) to afford meaningful differentiation among the eight syndrome scales. Except among 12-18-year-old girls scored on the TRF, 30 is below the borderline clinical range for total problem scores on the CBCL, TRF, and YSR. Some children whose total problem scores are not clinically deviant and who have no syndrome scores in the clinical range may nevertheless be eligible for computation of ICCs between their profile and the relevant profile types. If users wish to restrict profile classification to children who are deviant according to their total problem scores, scores on particular syndromes, or some other criterion (such as clinical referral), they may choose to exclude children who do not meet such criteria. The cutpoint of ≥ 30 was merely chosen to provide a psychometrically sound basis for measuring similarity among profiles, rather than implying clinical deviance.

Like the taxonic use of syndromes, the profile types can be used for classification on the basis of data from a single informant, or on the basis of data from any combination of parent-, teacher-, and self-reports, as illustrated in the following sections.

Single Sources of Profile Data

If data are available from only a single informant, such as a parent, teacher, or youth, decisions about classification according to profile types must be made solely on the basis of that one source of data. If the child's total problem score is ≥ 30, the appropriate computer program will print out the ICCs between the child's profile and each of the relevant profile types. The ICCs will also be stored in the data file created by the program. As detailed in Chapter 4, we have used ICC = .445 as the basis for classifying children according to a profile type. This cutpoint was chosen because it is statistically significant at $p \leq .05$ (by one-tail test). Chapter 6 reports correlates of classification based on ICCs $\geq .445$ with profile types, but some users may wish to consider a particular child as resembling a type only if the ICC is higher. Other users may wish to consider lower ICCs, such as .35 or .40, as indicating sufficient similarity to be at least somewhat informative.

Because the profile types are not mutually exclusive, it is possible for a child to have ICCs ≥.445 with more than one type. The user can then decide whether to consider the child as matching primarily the type for which the ICC is highest. On the other hand, if there is little difference between the child's highest ICCs, the user can apply data regarding correlates of both types to evaluation of the child. Significant ICCs with more than one profile type are most likely to be found when neither ICC is very large and when both types have some similar features. For example, a child might have an ICC of .490 with the Aggressive-Delinquent type and .445 with the Delinquent type scored from the CBCL. Information previously accumulated about both types might be relevant to evaluation of the child.

In studies where children are classified according to profile types scored from a single source, the researcher can choose a convention for classifying children who have significant ICCs with more than one type. The simplest procedure is to assign children to the types with which they have the highest ICCs, even if some have a second highest ICC that is only slightly lower. However, if it is important to distinguish as clearly as possible among those assigned to different types, children having two ICCs within a designated interval can be excluded. For example, we might choose to exclude children who have significant ICCs with two profile types if the ICCs differ by less than .100.

Multiple Sources of Profile Data

As described in Chapter 4, we identified four profile types whose centroids correlated significantly among the CBCL, TRF, and YSR. These *cross-informant profile types* are designated as *Withdrawn, Somatic Complaints, Social Problems*, and *Delinquent-Aggressive*. The four cross-informant types provide the main foci for applications of multisource data to taxonomies of profile types.

Although the cross-informant types reflect similarities in profile patterns that we found in ratings by different informants, this does not necessarily mean that a particular child would be classified by the same type according to all informants. In fact, we have found only modest agreement between categorical classifications of children according to ICCs ≥.445 with profile types scored from different informants. Phi correlations have shown significant agreement between profile types scored from pairs of parents, pairs of teachers, and the various combinations of different types of informants, but these phi correlations ranged only up to .42. (A phi correlation is a Pearson r computed on categorical data; in this case the phi correlations reflected the degree of agreement between categorizations of profiles scored from pairs of informants.) The highest phi was for agreement between mothers and fathers in classifying 154 boys and girls according to the Social Problems-Attention Problems profile type that is specific to the CBCL for ages 12-18. Among the four cross-informant profile types, the highest phi was .36 for classification according to the Withdrawn profile type by pairs of teachers.

In contrast to the low phi correlations for cross-informant categorical agreement, Pearson rs up to .65 were found between the ICCs of the profile types with profiles scored from the same informant pairs for whom the categorical agreements were computed. For example, we computed the ICCs between a particular profile type and profiles scored from CBCLs completed by mothers. We also computed the ICCs between the same profile types and profiles scored from fathers' CBCLs. We then computed the Pearson r between the ICCs obtained from the mothers' CBCLs and the ICCs obtained from their spouses' CBCLs. The highest Pearson r obtained between the ICCs for any pairing of informants like this was .65 between the ICCs that the profiles scored from 411 mother-father pairs had with the Delinquent-Aggressive type.

The level of agreement for classification according to profile type is affected by two aspects of the profiles obtained from each informant. These are *(1)* the overall *elevation* of the child's syndrome scales (i.e., how high or low the scale scores are); and *(2)* the *shape* of the child's profile pattern (i.e., the elevation of each scale score relative to the child's other seven scales). Thus, the profiles scored from two informants may both have shapes similar to that of a particular profile type. However, if their *elevations* differ much, it is possible that only one of the profiles will achieve an ICC ≥.445 with the profile type. Conversely, profiles scored from two informants may both have elevations similar to that of a particular profile type. Yet, if their *shapes* differ much, it is possible that only one may achieve an ICC ≥.445 with the type. Furthermore, even though the profile types are designated by the scales on which they have their peaks, the scales on which they are low contribute just as much to the definition of the type. Consequently, a child's profile may have peaks like those on a profile type, but if the child's profile differs much in its pattern of scores on the other scales, it may not achieve an ICC ≥.445 with the type.

In short, a profile represents a complex configuration of information. Even though a profile scored from one informant shares some elements with a profile type or a profile scored from another informant, there are multiple reasons why it may fail to reach the taxonomic criterion of ICC ≥.445. To deal with the fact that agreement is seldom very high, the following sections present some categorical and quantitative approaches to using multisource data to classify children according to profile types.

Multisource Categorical Classification by Profile Types. The simplest classification procedure is to identify children whose profiles have significant ICCs with the same profile type in each available source of data. For example, a child whose profile correlated ≥.445 with the Somatic

Complaints type on the CBCL, TRF, and YSR would be clearly classifiable by that type.

Users can adopt their own criteria for classification according to the cross-informant profile types. The most stringent criterion would be to classify children according to a profile type only if ICCs $\geq$.445 were obtained between that type and the profiles scored from each of several informants. Such a stringent criterion would ensure that children so classified would appear quite similar to all informants.

However, there are many reasons why at least one informant's ratings may not yield an ICC $\geq$.445 even though ratings by other informants do. Because this is a categorical criterion, an ICC of even .444 from one informant would disqualify a child from classification according to a particular type, if we required categorical agreement among all informants. To take account of possible anomalies in ratings by particular informants, as well as situation-specific variations in children's behavior, a less than unanimous criterion can be employed. For example, if both parents, two teachers, and a youth all rated the youth, we could choose to classify the youth according to a profile type if the ICCs from 3 or 4 informants were $\geq$.445.

Quantifying Multisource Classification by Profile Types. Because the ICC measures the similarity of each profile type to profiles scored from particular informants, ICCs of each type with profiles from different informants can be averaged to determine which type a child most closely resembles. If the mean ICC is $\geq$.445 with a particular profile type, this would be evidence of significant similarity to that type.

Because the profile types have just been developed, it is not yet known which approaches to cross-informant profile classification will be most effective for what purposes. Chapter 6 presents correlates of profile types found to date, but it is expected that users will test many other correlates in diverse ways. At the moment, one of the greatest contributions of the profile types may be in revealing the most common patterns of relations among syndromes, as seen by different informants.

The cross-informant types designated by elevations on single syndromes (Withdrawn, Somatic Complaints, Social Problems) indicate that significant numbers of referred children who are more deviant than their referred peers on these single syndromes tend to be less deviant than their referred peers on some other syndromes, as shown by the centroids in Figures 4-4 to 4-6. The Delinquent-Aggressive type indicates that a substantial number of referred children tend to be more deviant in both these areas than on other syndromes. Yet, the Delinquent type that is specific to the CBCL and the one specific to girls on the YSR indicate that some children manifest considerable deviant behavior on the Delinquent Behavior syndrome without being very deviant on the Aggressive Behavior syndrome. Furthermore, the Withdrawn-Anxious/Depressed-Aggressive profile found for boys on the CBCL represents a group that is quite deviant on the Aggressive Behavior syndrome, plus two other syndromes, without being so deviant on the Delinquent Behavior syndrome.

The profile types that have multiple peaks indicate that some children share more complex patterns of problems than implied by classification according to single syndromes or diagnostic categories. The empirical identification of profile types is a step toward conceptualizing the complex configurations that may occur.

RELATIONS BETWEEN SYNDROME- AND PROFILE-BASED TAXONOMIES

The foregoing sections described several ways to use syndromes and profile types to form taxonomic groupings. The syndrome-based taxonomies identify children according to their deviance on specific sets of problems. A child can be deviant on any one or more of the eight cross-informant syndromes. Ratings by different informants or by the same informant on different occasions may yield deviant scores on different syndromes. For both clinical and research purposes, users may focus on each syndrome by itself in the same way that they might focus on DSM diagnostic categories. Thus, for example, if users are interested in treating or studying attentional problems, they may look for children who are deviant on the Attention Problems syndrome, just as they might also look for children who qualify for a DSM diagnosis of ADHD.

A basic difference between the empirically based syndromes and the DSM categories is that—unlike DSM categories—each syndrome is not necessarily assumed to represent a separate disorder. A child who is deviant on both the Attention Problems and Aggressive Behavior syndromes, for example, is not necessarily assumed to have two separate comorbid disorders, whereas a child who qualifies for DSM diagnoses of ADHD and CD is assumed to have two separate disorders.

Because the empirically based syndromes are viewed as descriptions of co-occurring problems, rather than as discrete disorders, the particular pattern of scores on all syndromes may capture useful information not captured by each syndrome taken one-by-one. The profile types were derived to identify patterns that are shared by enough children to warrant being tested as an additional basis for taxonomy. However, even though the profile types reflect patterns of syndrome scores, they do not supersede the syndromes as a basis for judging deviance or the particular kinds of problems in which deviance is manifested. Instead, profile types and syndrome scores can be used separately or together for both clinical and research purposes. Until more is known about the correlates of the profile types, it is likely that syndrome scores will continue to be the primary focus in most cases. Profile types, on the other hand, will probably be used for specialized clinical and research purposes to provide additional information on those cases that correlate significantly with particular types.

SUMMARY

There are multiple ways to use the empirically based syndromes and profile types to form taxonomic groupings. When ratings are available from only one informant, children can be classified as deviant versus nondeviant on each syndrome according to whether their scores are above or below a clinical cutpoint. This dichotomous classification can be changed to a trichotomous classification by using the borderline range to identify children who are less clearly classifiable as deviant versus nondeviant than those whose scores are well above or below the cutpoint.

The continuous syndrome scores can be used taxometrically to measure the degree to which a child manifests the problems of a syndrome. Discriminant analyses can be used to combine multiple syndrome scores from a single source to assign children to taxa.

When syndrome data are available from multiple sources, a *taxonomic decision tree* can be used to identify children who are deviant on a single syndrome according to all sources, those who are deviant on a particular combination of syndromes according to all sources, and those for whom there are major inconsistencies among sources.

Continuous syndrome scores from multiple sources can be used taxonically by averaging standard scores obtained from all sources and by using MANOVA or discriminant analysis to form weighted combinations of continuous scores.

The empirically based profile types embody patterns of syndrome scores that have been found to classify subsamples of clinically referred children. Unlike the syndromes, the profiles do not have cutpoints for discriminating between the normal and clinical range. Instead, they provide a basis for grouping children according to the overall pattern of their syndrome scores. To ensure meaningful differentiation among scale scores, only children who obtain total problem raw scores ≥30 are eligible to have ICCs computed to measure resemblance to the profile types. Achieving a significant ICC of ≥.445 with a profile type does not by itself indicate clinical deviance but only that the child's profile is similar to that type. Children may have a high ICC with a type but not be very deviant. Conversely, children may have no significant ICCs with any profile type, but have high problem scores.

When ratings are available from only one informant, children can be classified according to profile types on the basis of ICC ≥.445 or other cutpoints chosen by users. If ratings from multiple informants are available, users can choose to require unanimous or less than unanimous agreement in profile classification. The ICCs from multiple informants can also be averaged to determine whether the mean ICC with a particular type is ≥.445.

The syndromes and profiles provide different kinds of taxonomic possibilities that are complementary rather than being mutually exclusive. Each syndrome provides an indication of deviance with respect to a particular grouping of problems for every child. The profile types, by contrast, are defined by complex combinations of elevations and configurations of syndrome scores. Many children manifest profile patterns that do not correlate significantly with any of the types identified to date.

Chapter 6
Correlates of Empirically Based Taxa

The preceding chapters presented the development of empirically based syndromes and profile types, plus relations between various approaches to empirically based taxonomy. This chapter presents a sampling of research on the correlates and theoretical implications of the empirically based taxa. Over a thousand publications report use of our instruments (Brown & Achenbach, 1993). Many of these publications report new research findings. Because the findings are so diverse, the sampling presented here illustrates only a portion of the findings that are relevant to the taxonomic implications of specific syndromes and profile types.

Because the eight cross-informant syndromes were introduced only in 1991, relatively little research has been published on them to date. However, most of these syndromes correlate highly with syndromes derived previously from the CBCL, TRF, and YSR (Achenbach, 1991b, 1991c, 1991d, presents correlations between the 1991 and pre-1991 syndrome scales from each instrument). Research on the pre-1991 versions will therefore be presented when it is relevant to the 1991 versions. Findings are first presented for syndromes within the groupings designated as Internalizing and Externalizing, followed by the syndromes that do not belong to either of these groupings.

Because the profile types derived from the 1991 cross-informant syndromes are being introduced with this book, there is no previously published research. We therefore present initial findings on correlates of the new profile types, plus correlates of previous versions of the profile types that were similar to the present ones.

CORRELATES OF
INTERNALIZING SYNDROMES

The Internalizing grouping includes the syndromes designated as *Anxious/Depressed, Withdrawn*, and *Somatic Complaints*. Neither this grouping nor the Externalizing grouping imply that their constituent syndromes have similar etiologies. Instead, the two groupings comprise subsets of syndrome scales that loaded on different second-order factors. As detailed elsewhere (Achenbach, 1991a), the Internalizing and Externalizing groupings were derived from the mean loadings obtained by the syndrome scales in separate second-order factor analyses of each sex/age group scored on the CBCL, TRF, and YSR. The Internalizing grouping reflects the finding that scores on the Anxious/Depressed, Withdrawn, and Somatic Complaints syndromes correlate more highly with each other than with other syndromes. Similarly, the Externalizing grouping reflects the finding that scores on the Aggressive Behavior and Delinquent Behavior syndromes also correlated more highly with each other than with other syndromes.

Children who have high scores on one of the three Internalizing syndromes do not necessarily have high scores on the other two syndromes. Nor do children who have high scores on Internalizing syndromes necessarily have low scores on Externalizing syndromes. On the contrary, the mean r of .52 between the Internalizing score and the Externalizing score indicates a moderate positive association between them in our normative samples for the CBCL, TRF, and YSR (Achenbach, 1991a). Furthermore, as shown in Chapter 4, some profile types include elevations on both Internalizing and Externalizing scales. An example is the profile type designated as Withdrawn-Anxious/Depressed-Aggressive that was found for boys on the CBCL.

Because there are so many possible patterns of high and low scores, most children are not expected to be definitively classifiable as Internalizers versus Externalizers. Nevertheless, the problems comprising the Internalizing grouping tend to be similar in being within the self, in contrast to the conflicts with other people and violations of social mores comprising the Externalizing grouping.

It is possible that certain underlying variables contribute to the covariation among syndromes reflected in the Internalizing versus Externalizing groupings. For example, Internalizing problems may involve excessive anxiety, whereas Externalizing problems may involve deficient anxiety. However, even if a characteristic such as high or low anxiety is common to the problems of the Internalizing or Externalizing grouping, this may stem from a variety of sources and is unlikely to be the sole cause of the problems. In some cases, problems comprising one syndrome may lead to problems comprising another syndrome. It has been found, for example, that high scores on the Attention Problems syndrome predict later elevations on the Delinquent Behavior syndrome in some children (Stanger et al., 1992). Because so many causal and developmental relations are possible among the various kinds of problems, one of the main contributions of current research will be to provide clearer pictures of particular syndromes. This will enable us to form more specific hypotheses about differential etiologies, developmental courses, possible interventions, and likely outcomes.

The Anxious/Depressed Syndrome

Nosologies such as the DSM usually have separate categories for disorders characterized by anxiety versus depression. Yet, our principal components analyses of the CBCL, TRF, and YSR yielded a syndrome that included both kinds of problems rather than separate syndromes for anxiety and depression. As shown in Table 3-1, the

Anxious/Depressed syndrome includes items indicative of anxiety, such as *Too fearful or anxious* and *Nervous, highstrung, or tense*. It also includes items indicative of depression, such as *Unhappy, sad, or depressed* and *Feels worthless or inferior*. Other items of the syndrome, however, can be interpreted as involving either anxiety, depression, or both. Examples include *Cries a lot* and *Worries*. Still other items that might be interpreted as signs of anxiety and/or depression loaded more highly on other empirically derived syndromes, such as those designated as Somatic Complaints and Withdrawn. Examples include *Overtired, Feels dizzy, Headaches, Nausea,* and *Underactive, slow moving or lacks energy,*

Does the combination of problems indicative of both anxiety and depression in the same syndrome mean that an important distinction between disorders of anxiety and depression has been lost? Most people distinguish between *feelings* of anxiety and depression. However, a variety of research suggests considerable overlap between pathologically extreme forms of these affects, especially in children. The overlap between these affects is evident in the following ways: *(1)* certain problems may involve both anxiety and depression; *(2)* problems suggestive of anxiety tend to co-occur with problems suggestive of depression, even when separate measures are used for anxiety and depression (Finch, Lipovsky, & Casat, 1989); *(3)* longitudinal findings indicate that anxiety disorders may be followed by depressive disorders (Kovacs, Gatsonis, Paulauskas, & Richards, 1989); and *(4)* similar biological correlates have been found for anxiety and depression (Finch et al., 1989).

To deal with the lack of clear borders between anxiety and depression, it has been proposed that both are manifestations of *negative affectivity* (Watson & Clark, 1984). According to this view, some people have a general disposition to experience discomfort across diverse situations even in the absence of overt stress. This disposition is manifested in a variety of ways, including anxiety and depression. Although most people may experience anxiety or depression in response to external stressors, those who display persistent anxiety or depression not attributable to external stressors may share an underlying tendency toward negative affect that is not restricted to either anxiety or depression.

The covariation between problems of anxiety and depression reflected in the Anxious/Depressed syndrome does not imply that children cannot manifest primarily anxiety versus primarily depression, nor that the differences between these kinds of problems cannot be detected. Among children obtaining high scores on the Anxious/Depressed syndrome, some may have high scores mainly on the items indicative of anxiety. Other children may have high scores mainly on the items indicative of depression or on the items that might imply either anxiety or depression, such as *Cries a lot.*

Further research may clarify whether anxiety and depressive disorders should be considered distinct from each other, or whether there are more complex relations between them. One possibility is that anxiety and depression are more easily separated during some developmental periods than others. In the meantime, however, the combination of anxiety and depressive problems comprising the Anxious/Depressed syndrome corresponds to findings from many kinds of research. The following sections address other kinds of findings related to the Anxious/Depressed syndrome. Reflecting the recent popularity of child and adolescent depression as a research topic, most of the work has focused on depression, although it may be applicable to anxiety as well.

Affect, Syndrome, and Disorder. Nearly everybody experiences affective states construed as anxiety and depression. Such affects are not intrinsically pathological, especially in response to identifiable stressors, such as the loss of loved ones and threats to well-being. Nevertheless,

CBCL, TRF, and YSR items such as *Too fearful or anxious* and *Unhappy, sad, or depressed* are scored significantly higher for children referred for mental health services than for nonreferred children (Achenbach, 1991b, 1991c, 1991d). In fact, the item *Unhappy, sad, or depressed* is one of the strongest discriminators between referred and nonreferred children in parent-, teacher-, and self-reports. Not only are there large differences between the prevalence rates for referred versus nonreferred children, but this item is endorsed for as many as 80% of referred children.

Even though the mere occurrence of dysphoric affect is seldom a reason for referral, persistent or intense dysphoric affect often signifies maladjustment severe enough to warrant professional help. Nevertheless, dysphoric affect by itself is unlikely to signify the presence only of an anxiety disorder, a depressive disorder, or a combination of them. Instead, its power to discriminate between referred and nonreferred children may stem at least partly from the fact that it can result from a variety of conditions. Thus, for example, children who have poor social skills may become unhappy because they are rejected by others. In such cases, dysphoric affect may be an important indicator of need for help and may be an appropriate target for treatment in its own right, even if it is not a symptom of a depressive disorder as such. Because dysphoric affect is reported for so many troubled children and may occur for so many reasons, it is important to avoid automatically equating it with an affective disorder.

In addition to dysphoric affect, the problem items that comprise the Anxious/Depressed syndrome include a variety of other negative feelings and attitudes. For example, the YSR version of the Anxious/Depressed syndrome includes suicidal thoughts and behavior, while the TRF version includes *Overconforms to rules, Feels hurt when criticized, Overly anxious to please,* and *Is afraid of making mistakes.*

For taxonomic purposes, the sum of a child's scores on the items of the Anxious/Depressed syndrome is compared with scores obtained by normative samples of children of the same sex and age range to determine whether the child's problems are above or within the "normal" range—i.e., equivalent to a T score <67. Users can choose other cutpoints, such as the top of the borderline clinical range (T = 70), to categorically identify deviance. However, the syndrome score provides a continuous metric of the degree to which the problems of that syndrome are reported for the child. A high score on the syndrome does not necessarily indicate that the child has a "disorder," but only that a particular informant reports many of the problems comprising the syndrome.

The child's scores on other syndromes may indicate that the child is even more deviant in other areas. Or a significant ICC with a profile type such as the Withdrawn-Anxious/Depressed-Aggressive type for boys on the CBCL may indicate that high scores on the Anxious/Depressed syndrome contribute just one component of a profile pattern that is shared by other children.

Because deviance on a particular syndrome should not automatically be equated with a disorder, the judgment that a child needs help and the targeting of the help on particular areas of functioning should be based on all available information about the child. If better validated criteria are evolved for judging the presence of disorders, the relations between those criteria and scores on the Anxious/Depressed syndrome can be tested. It may then be found that cutpoints other than $T = 67$ and $T = 70$ yield better agreement with criteria for a disorder of depression and/or anxiety. Although such well-validated criteria for disorders do not yet exist, several studies have tested relations between our empirically based Anxious/Depressed syndrome and other criteria, as summarized in the following section.

Relations to Other Measures. Numerous procedures have been developed to assess anxiety and depression in the young. These include interviews, personality questionnaires, self-ratings of problems, and reports by informants. The difficulty of clearly distinguishing between constructs of anxiety and depression is evident in the inclusion of very similar items in measures of both constructs (King, Ollendick, & Gullone, 1991). For example, the Revised Children's Manifest Anxiety Scale (RCMAS; Reynolds & Richmond, 1978) includes "I often worry about something bad happening to me," which is very similar to "I worry that bad things will happen to me" on the Children's Depression Inventory (CDI; Kovacs, 1981).

In view of the similarity of content and the findings of high correlations between indices of anxiety and depression (Finch et al., 1989), we will not try to determine whether relations between our empirically based syndrome and other measures truly reflect anxiety or depression. To facilitate communication, we will adhere to the terminology of the authors who reported the findings. However, at our present stage of knowledge, it may be less confusing to think in terms of negative or dysphoric affect, rather than assigning each finding to separate categories of anxiety versus depression. Despite the importance of conceptually distinguishing between affects, syndromes, and disorders (Compas, Ey, & Grant, 1993), existing measures have not operationally discriminated between these levels of disturbance. We will therefore consider the findings without regard to whether they are restricted to affects, syndromes, or disorders.

Using Receiver (also called "Relative") Operating Characteristics (ROC) analyses, Rey and Morris-Yates (1992) tested relations between DSM diagnoses of Major Depression made from case history data and empirically derived CBCL and YSR syndromes scored for clinically referred Australian adolescents. They found that both the pre-1991 Depressed syndrome and the 1991 Anxious/Depressed syndrome scored from the YSR discriminated very well between adolescents who met criteria for Major Depression versus other disorders. Combining CBCL and YSR data improved discrimination still further. Rey and Morris-Yates concluded that diagnoses of depression in adolescents were as strongly associated with both CBCL and YSR syndrome scores as are diagnoses of depression in adults with the Dexamethasone Suppression Test, which is one of the most studied biomedical tests for depression.

In addition to the significant relations to DSM diagnoses of depression made from case histories, the empirically based syndromes have also been found to relate significantly to DSM diagnoses made independently from diagnostic interviews. In one study, the CBCL and the parent version of the Diagnostic Interview Schedule for Children (DISC-P) were administered to parents of clinically referred 6- to 16-year-olds (Edelbrock & Costello, 1988). Scores on the pre-1991 version of the CBCL Depressed syndrome were significantly associated with diagnoses of Major Depression and Dysthymia, which Edelbrock and Costello combined because all children who met criteria for Major Depression also met criteria for Dysthymia. Significant relations were found in analyses that preserved the quantitative nature of the syndrome scores and the categorical nature of the diagnoses. These analyses included point-biserial correlations and a linear trend analysis that showed a steady increase in the proportion of children receiving diagnoses of depression/dysthymia within each successive 5-point interval of T scores on the Depressed syndrome scale.

Edelbrock and Costello also analyzed quantitative variations in diagnostic criteria by forming groups of children who failed to meet DSM criteria for depression/dysthymia, those who just met the minimum criteria (designated as mild cases), and those who exceeded the minimum criteria (designated as severe cases). As Figure 6-1 shows, children who failed to meet the diagnostic criteria obtained mean CBCL T scores below 65, whereas those who were classified as mild cases obtained mean T scores above 70, and those classified as severe cases had still higher T scores.

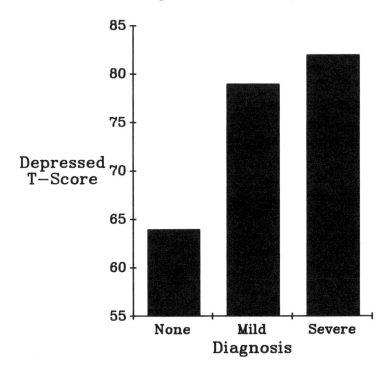

Figure 6-1. Mean *T* scores on pre-1991 CBCL Depressed syndrome for children who failed to meet DSM criteria, just met DSM criteria, or exceeded DSM criteria for Depression or Dysthymia. (Reproduced by permission from Edelbrock & Costello, 1988, p. 228.)

In another study, the DISC was administered to adolescent inpatients who also completed the YSR (Weinstein, Noam, Grimes, Stone, & Schwab-Stone, 1990). Self-ratings on the pre-1991 YSR Depressed syndrome were significantly higher among adolescents who qualified for DSM diagnoses of affective and anxiety disorders than among adolescents who did not.

Significant agreement has also been found between the empirically based scales and measures that were not structured according to DSM criteria. For example, the pre-1991 CBCL Depressed syndrome scored from parents' ratings was found to correlate .51 with scores on the

Depression symptom complex of a semistructured clinical interview administered to children, the Child Assessment Schedule (CAS; Hodges, Kline, Stern, Cytryn, & McKnew, 1982). In addition, significant correlations have been found between TRF Internalizing scores and self-report measures of depression and anxiety, including the Children's Depression Inventory, the Revised Children's Manifest Anxiety Scale, and the State-Trait Anxiety Inventory for Children (Wolfe, Blount, Finch, Saylor, Pallmeyer, & Carek, 1984).

Relations to Maternal Depression. Several studies have reported positive associations between CBCL problem scores and depression in the mothers who completed the CBCLs (e.g., Conrad & Hammen, 1989; Friedlander, Weiss, & Traylor, 1986; Richters & Pellegrini, 1989). This raises the question of whether problems such as those of the Anxious/Depressed syndrome reflect the rater's own affective state. However, the findings of associations between maternal depression and CBCL scores are subject to a variety of interpretations, including the following: *(1)* high problem scores on CBCLs completed by depressed mothers reflect the mothers' distorted perceptions of their children's problems (the *depression→distortion hypothesis*); *(2)* children of depressed mothers really do have high rates of problems because *(a)* they share their mothers' constitutional vulnerabilities to depressive disorders, *(b)* the children's elevated problems are responses to stress imposed by depressed mothers, or *(c)* maternal depression and the children's elevated problems are both reactions to a common stressor, such as abusive fathers; and *(3)* mothers' depression may be a response to their children's elevated problems.

In a comprehensive review of the relevant research, Richters (1992) concluded that "None of the studies that claimed evidence for a depression→distortion influence on mothers' ratings of their children met the necessary and sufficient criteria for establishing distortion" (p. 485).

Instead, in those studies that analyzed agreement with other types of informants, such as teachers and observers, depressed mothers agreed with the criterion informants at least as well as nondepressed mothers did.

There is considerable evidence from sources other than their parents that children of depressed parents do in fact have more problems than children whose parents are not depressed. In addition, the association between mothers' depression and their reports of their children's problems may not be specific to depression, as maternal depression has been found to correlate with many other maternal and child problems (e.g., Jensen, Traylor, Xenakis, & Davis, 1988). Thus, beside the lack of support for the depression→ distortion hypothesis, the positive association between maternal depression and children's problems may reflect a general relation between diverse maternal and child problems.

The findings for reports by mothers are likely to apply to reports by fathers and other informants as well. That is, reports by particular informants may be correlated with characteristics of those informants, but positive associations between informants' problems such as depression and the problems they report for children should not be automatically dismissed as distortions. Such associations may contribute important information about the children, the informants, and relations between them.

The Withdrawn Syndrome

Much of the research related to the Anxious/Depressed syndrome has been inspired by the popularity of child and adolescent depression as a topic. Perhaps because the problems of the Withdrawn syndrome have not attracted as much attention, there has been far less research related to it. Among the DSM categories, the closest analogue to the Withdrawn syndrome appears to be Avoidant Disorder of Childhood or Adolescence, which does not have detailed defining criteria and has not been the subject of much research. On the other hand, there has been considerable research on shyness and withdrawal as traits of temperament (e.g., Kagan, Gibbons, Johnson, Reznick, & Snidman, 1990). Measures of these traits often include characteristics like some of the problem items comprising the Withdrawn syndrome, shown in Table 3-1.

Despite the relative lack of research related to the Withdrawn syndrome, it is likely to represent an important aspect of children's functioning. For example, one of the cross-informant profile types is characterized by high scores on the Withdrawn syndrome and relatively low scores on the other syndromes, as shown in Figures 4-4 to 4-6. Furthermore, scores on the Withdrawn syndrome discriminate strongly between referred and nonreferred children in parent-, teacher-, and self-ratings (Achenbach, 1991b, 1991c, 1991d). Scores on this syndrome are also moderately stable over long periods, as indicated by a 3-year stability $r = .48$ between parents' ratings of the Withdrawn syndrome in a national sample of American children (McConaughy et al., 1992) and a 6-year stability $r = .43$ in a general population sample of Dutch children (Verhulst & van der Ende, 1992).

Path analyses over a 3-year period have shown that initial scores on the Withdrawn syndrome significantly predicted outcome scores on the Withdrawn syndrome after partialling out other predictors (Stanger et al., 1992). In addition, initial scores on the Withdrawn syndrome had a significant *negative* association with outcome scores on the Aggressive Behavior syndrome. That is, children who had *high* initial scores on the Withdrawn syndrome tended to have *low* scores on the Aggressive Behavior syndrome 3 years later. This indicates that the problems of the Withdrawn syndrome tend to work against the development of aggressive behavior.

Comparisons of correlations between scores for monozygotic (identical) versus dizygotic (fraternal) twins have yielded a highly significant heritability estimate of .59 for the Withdrawn syndrome scored from the CBCL (Edelbrock,

Rende, Plomin, & Thompson, 1993). There was no evidence for within-family environmental influences on the CBCL Withdrawn scores. Problems of the Withdrawn syndrome thus appear to have trait-like qualities, although the magnitude of the long-term stabilities and of the genetic effects also leave considerable room for developmental change and nongenetic effects.

The Somatic Complaints Syndrome

The remaining Internalizing syndrome resembles the DSM diagnostic category of Somatization Disorder. Although the DSM indicates no minimum age, it does not list Somatization Disorder with disorders usually first evident in infancy, childhood, and adolescence. Furthermore, the DSM-III-R Manual states that "Symptoms usually begin in the teen years or, rarely, in the 20s" (American Psychiatric Association, 1987, p. 262).

The implication that Somatization Disorder does not occur prior to adolescence may account for the lack of research on it in children. However, our analyses have identified a clear-cut syndrome comprising somatic problems without known medical cause across both sexes and all the ages spanned by the CBCL/4-18, TRF, and YSR. We have also derived a fairly similar syndrome for ages 2 and 3 from the CBCL/2-3 (Achenbach, 1992). These findings argue against the implication that children do not manifest disorders like the DSM Somatization Disorder.

Instead of a childhood disorder characterized by somatic complaints without known medical cause, the DSM includes "somatic complaints, such as headaches or stomachaches, for which no physical basis can be established" among the criteria for Overanxious Disorder (American Psychiatric Association, 1987, p. 64). In analyzing relations between CBCL syndromes and DSM diagnoses made from the DISC-P, Edelbrock and Costello (1988) found that children who met criteria for Overanxious Disorder scored significantly higher on the CBCL Somatic Complaints syndrome than did children who failed to meet criteria for Overanxious Disorder.

Despite DSM's implied exclusion of children from Somatization Disorder, a comparison of 7- to 17-year-olds having abdominal pain from organic causes with those having abdominal pain with no detectible organic cause showed that the latter group had significantly higher scores on the CBCL Somatic Complaints syndrome (Routh & Ernst, 1984). The difference on the CBCL was quite specific to the Somatic Complaints syndrome, as the groups did not differ significantly on any other CBCL problem scale. Furthermore, among the 20 subjects whose abdominal pain resulted from a known organic cause, only one had a first- or second-degree relative who met DSM criteria for Somatization Disorder. This was significantly less than the 10 out of 20 subjects in the nonorganic group who had relatives meeting criteria for Somatization Disorder. The Somatic Complaints syndrome thus identified children and young adolescents whose problems were like those of the DSM Somatization Disorder. Moreover, the families of these children also had high rates of DSM Somatization Disorder.

The familial genetic vulnerability to somatization suggested by Routh and Ernst's findings is consistent with the .65 heritability found for the Somatic Complaints syndrome by Edelbrock et al. (1993). This heritability estimate was higher than for any other syndrome except Social Problems, for which the heritability estimate was also .65.

Other research has demonstrated a significant correlation between parents' ratings on the CBCL Somatic Complaints syndrome and self-ratings on the Children's Somatization Inventory, which was developed to assess somatic symptoms not attributable to organic disorders (Walker, Garber, & Greene, 1991). Furthermore, even after partialling out measures of pain, children with migraine headaches scored significantly higher on the CBCL Somatic Complaints syndrome than did children suffering pain from musculoskeletal abnormalities or a no-pain control group (Cunningham et al., 1987).

CORRELATES OF
EXTERNALIZING SYNDROMES

The Externalizing grouping includes the *Aggressive Behavior* and *Delinquent Behavior* syndromes. Most versions of the pre-1991 version of the Externalizing grouping also included the forerunner of the Attention Problems syndrome, which was designated as Hyperactive in most sex/age groups. However, in our separate second-order factor analyses of the eight cross-informant syndromes for each sex/age group scored on the CBCL, TRF, and YSR, we found that the Attention Problems syndrome had a mean loading of .62 on the Externalizing factor. The Aggressive Behavior syndrome had a mean loading of .79 and the Delinquent Behavior syndrome had a mean loading of .78 on this factor. Even though the Attention Problems syndrome was more strongly associated with the Externalizing grouping than with the Internalizing grouping, its loading was enough lower than the loadings of the Aggressive and Delinquent syndromes to warrant omitting it from the Externalizing grouping.

The separation of the Attention Problems syndrome from the Externalizing grouping is consistent with a growing differentiation in perspectives on these problems. It is increasingly recognized, for example, that children whose attention problems are accompanied by conduct problems may differ in important ways from children whose attention problems are not accompanied by conduct problems (e.g., Biederman, Newcorn, & Sprich, 1991). Thus, some children who are deviant on the Attention Problems syndrome may either concurrently or subsequently manifest problems of the Aggressive or Delinquent syndromes, but others may not manifest these problems.

The Externalizing grouping encompasses problems like those included in the DSM categories of Oppositional Defiant Disorder (ODD) and Conduct Disorder (CD). However, these two DSM categories divide problem behaviors differently than do the empirically based syndromes. ODD is defined mostly by problems like those of the Aggressive Behavior syndrome, including "often loses temper" and "often argues with adults" (American Psychiatric Association, 1987, p. 57). However, the DSM-III-R version of ODD also included "often swears or uses obscene language," which is included in the empirically based Delinquent syndrome.

CD mixes problems from both the Aggressive and Delinquent syndromes. For example, it includes fighting and cruelty to others, which were found to load on the Aggressive syndrome. And it includes stealing, running away from home, lying, truancy, and fire-setting, which were found to load on the Delinquent syndrome. Within its CD category, DSM-III-R permitted a distinction between *Group Type*, defined as "the predominance of conduct problems occurring mainly as a group activity with peers" versus *Solitary Aggressive Type*, defined as "the predominance of aggressive physical behavior, usually toward both adults and peers, initiated by the person (not as a group activity)" (p. 56).

Even though the Solitary Aggressive Type nominally refers to aggression, the distinction between it and the Group Type is not based on the presence of aggressive behavior. In fact, the definition of the Group Type states that "Aggressive physical behavior may or may not be present" (p. 56). Thus, neither the subtypes of CD nor the difference between ODD and CD correspond directly to the difference between overt aggression versus violations of social mores without overt aggression found in the empirically based Aggressive versus Delinquent syndromes. Furthermore, because only 3 out of 13 criteria must be met for a DSM diagnosis of CD, a child manifesting 3 aggressive problems, and a child manifesting 3 unaggressive problems would both qualify for the same diagnosis of CD.

In the following sections on the Aggressive and Delinquent syndromes, it is important to remember that the distinction between them does not correspond directly to the DSM distinction among ODD and Group versus Solitary Aggressive CD. Instead, our distinction rests on findings of different subsets of conduct problems that tend to co-occur, as reported by different kinds of informants in many studies beside our own (e.g., Hewitt & Jenkins, 1946; Jenkins & Boyer, 1968; Loeber & Schmaling, 1985; Quay, 1986).

The Aggressive Behavior Syndrome

Problem behaviors like those of the Aggressive Behavior syndrome have been found to co-occur in many samples of children, as reported by different informants and analyzed in different ways. In fact, reviews of empirically based taxonomic research have indicated that this is probably the most universally found syndrome (Achenbach, 1992; Quay, 1986). Furthermore, longitudinal studies show marked stabilities in children's rank orders on the Aggressive syndrome among peers of the same sex and age. In our national sample, for instance, the 3-year stability r was .58, while in the Dutch general population sample the 6-year stability r was .55 (McConaughy et al., 1992; Verhulst & van der Ende, 1992).

Although not specifically involving the empirically based syndrome, significant correlations have been found between peer nominations for aggression at age 8 and several measures of aggression at age 30 (Eron & Huesmann, 1990). Teacher ratings of aggression at age 10 have also been found to significantly predict criminal offenses recorded up to age 26 in a Swedish longitudinal study (Stattin & Magnusson, 1989).

The long-term stability and predictive power of aggressive behavior suggests that it has a trait-like quality.

Genetic studies of the Aggressive Behavior syndrome scored from the CBCL have yielded a heritability estimate of .94 for 4- to 7-year-old twins (Ghodsian-Carpey & Baker, 1987) and .50 for 7- to 15-year-old twins (Edelbrock et al., 1993). A comparison of adopted biological siblings, nonbiological siblings, and singletons scored on the Dutch CBCL also yielded significant heritability for the Aggressive Behavior syndrome (Van Den Oord, Boomsma, & Verhulst, 1993).

The genetic findings are consistent with the hypothesis of biological influences on the Aggressive Behavior syndrome. Based on Gray's (1982, 1987a, 1987b) theory of the Behavioral Inhibition System (BIS) and Behavioral Reward System (REW), Quay (1993) has hypothesized that the BIS is less active in individuals with aggressive conduct disorders than in other individuals. In addition, behavioral studies reviewed by Quay indicate that individuals with aggressive conduct disorders perseverate excessively in responding to ostensible reward. Quay has interpreted the findings as suggesting a greater dominance of the REW system, as well as a weaker BIS, in individuals manifesting persistent aggressive behavior.

Direct evidence of biological correlates of the Aggressive Behavior syndrome has been obtained in two studies of children with severe conduct disorders (Birmaher, Stanley, Greenhill, Twomey, Gavrilescu, & Rabinovich, 1990; Stoff, Pollock, Vitiello, Behar, & Bridger, 1987). Birmaher et al. obtained $r = -.50$ between scores on the CBCL Aggressive syndrome and a measure of imipramine binding, while Stoff et al. obtained $r = -.72$ between these two variables. The most aggressive children in both studies had the lowest levels of serotonergic activity. These findings are consistent with the theory that low serotonergic activity is quantitatively related to pathological aggression (Brown & van Praag, 1991).

The Delinquent Behavior Syndrome

The Delinquent syndrome correlates highly enough with the Aggressive syndrome to yield similar mean loadings of .78 and .79 for the two syndromes on the second-order Externalizing factor. Furthermore, as shown in Chapter 4, a cross-informant profile type was obtained that has peaks on both the Delinquent and Aggressive syndromes. It is thus clear that some children who are deviant on one of these syndromes are also deviant on the other one as well. Nevertheless, most children who are deviant on one syndrome are not deviant on the other. For example, the comorbidity between deviant scores on the Delinquent and Aggressive syndromes averaged across parent-, teacher-, and self-ratings was 28% in our nationally representative sample and 45% in demographically similar clinical samples (McConaughy & Achenbach, 1993). Moreover, as shown in Chapter 4, some profile types, such as the CBCL Withdrawn-Anxious/Depressed-Aggressive type for boys, are characterized by a peak on only one of the two Externalizing syndromes.

In contrast to the evidence that the Aggressive syndrome represents a quite stable trait over long periods of development, the Delinquent syndrome appears to be developmentally more variable. In our national sample, the 3-year stability $r = .44$ for Delinquent Behavior was significantly lower than the $r = .58$ for Aggressive Behavior (McConaughy et al., 1992). The 6-year stability $r = .36$ for the Delinquent syndrome was also significantly lower than the stability $r = .55$ for the Aggressive syndrome in the Dutch general population sample (Verhulst & van der Ende, 1992).

Accelerated longitudinal analyses of the Dutch data showed higher 4- and 6-year *between-cohort* and *within-cohort* correlations for Aggressive Behavior than Delinquent Behavior (Stanger, Achenbach, & Verhulst, 1993). To obtain between-cohort correlations, children from one cohort were matched with children from another cohort for their initial Aggressive Behavior scores. Similar between-cohort matching was done on the basis of the Delinquent Behavior scores. The correlations between initial scores by children in one cohort with later scores obtained by their matched partners were then found to be significantly higher for Aggressive Behavior than for Delinquent Behavior. For Delinquent Behavior, the longitudinal stabilities were significantly lower for girls and younger children than for boys and older children, whereas the stabilities for Aggressive Behavior did not differ by sex or age. In a variety of ways, the findings from these accelerated longitudinal analyses thus demonstrated more trait-like stability for the Aggressive than the Delinquent syndrome across multiple birth cohorts, ages, SES, and both sexes.

In their twin study of genetic effects on the syndromes, Edelbrock et al. (1993) obtained a significant but considerably lower heritability estimate of .29 for the Delinquent syndrome than the heritability estimate of .50 for the Aggressive syndrome. Conversely, Edelbrock et al. found a larger effect of shared environment for the Delinquent syndrome than for the Aggressive syndrome (.37 versus .15). In their study of siblings, Van Den Oord et al. (1993) also obtained a lower heritability estimate for the Delinquent than the Aggressive syndrome.

On a behavioral level, Quay (1993) has reviewed research indicating that—unlike more aggressive youths— youths with delinquent conduct problems do not differ from other unaggressive youths in moral reasoning, abstract reasoning, empathy, stimulus seeking, or psychophysiological responses. It has also been found that unaggressive delinquent youths adapt better than aggressive youths to institutional settings and have better outcomes after release (Henn, Bardwell, & Jenkins, 1980). Multiple kinds of evidence thus indicate that the Delinquent and Aggressive syndromes are likely to have different determinants and developmental courses, despite their co-occurrence in some children.

CORRELATES OF SYNDROMES
NOT CLASSIFIED AS
INTERNALIZING OR EXTERNALIZING

As discussed earlier, the Attention Problems syndrome had a moderately high mean loading of .62 on the second-order factor on which the Aggressive and Delinquent syndromes loaded .79 and .78, respectively. The Social Problems and Thought Problems syndromes were not as strongly associated with either the Internalizing or External-izing syndromes. The mean loading of the Social Problems syndrome was .50 on the Internalizing factors and .48 on the Externalizing factors derived from different sex/age groups on the CBCL, TRF, and YSR. The mean loading of the Thought Problems syndrome was .43 on the Internalizing factors and .54 on the Externalizing factors.

The Attention Problems, Social Problems, and Thought Problems syndromes do not constitute a third grouping of mutually associated syndromes analogous to the Internalizing and Externalizing syndromes. Instead, deviant scores on these syndromes are almost equally likely to occur in combination with most of the other syndromes. As described in Chapter 4, high scores on these syndromes also help to define some of the empirically derived profile types. Our illustrations of correlates start with the Attention Problems syndrome because it has been the subject of much more research than the Social Problems and Thought Problems syndromes.

The Attention Problems Syndrome

This syndrome includes several items similar to those that define the DSM categories designated as Attention Deficit Disorder in DSM-III, Attention Deficit Hyperactivity

Disorder in DSM-III-R, and Attention Deficit/Hyperactivity Disorder(s) in DSM-IV (American Psychiatric Association, 1980, 1987, 1993). To warrant a diagnosis, DSM-III required descriptive features from three different subcategories, whereas DSM-III-R provided only a single category of descriptive features. DSM-IV provides two subcategories of features, but a diagnosis can be made if a child displays a sufficient number of features from either of the two subcategories. Despite the enormous volume of research on such disorders, the major shifts from DSM-III to DSM-III-R and then to DSM-IV reflect the continuing lability of the diagnostic constructs.

Empirically based multivariate analyses have identified a syndrome resembling our Attention Problems syndrome in at least 22 samples (Achenbach, 1992). The Attention Problems syndrome has been found to correlate significantly with versions from other instruments. For example, the CBCL Attention Problems syndrome correlated .77 with parents' ratings of the Attention Problems scale of the Quay-Peterson (1983) Revised Behavior Problem Checklist (Achenbach, 1991b). Similarly, the 1991 TRF Attention Problems syndrome has correlated .80 with the Inattentive Passive score of the Conners Revised Teacher Rating Scale (Achenbach, 1991c; Goyette, Conners, & Ulrich, 1978). The 1991 versions of our Attention Problems syndrome also maintain considerable continuity with earlier versions, as indicated by rs of .88 to .95 with their pre-1991 counterparts on the CBCL and .97 to .99 on the TRF (Achenbach, 1991b, 1991c; there was no pre-1991 version for the YSR).

Like the Aggressive Behavior syndrome, the Attention Problems syndrome shows trait-like qualities, including relatively high stability rs of .57 over 3 years, .56 over 4 years, and .44 over 6 years (McConaughy et al., 1992; Verhulst & van der Ende, 1992). The Attention Problems syndrome yielded a heritability estimate of .64 in a twin study and .58 in a study of adoptees (Edelbrock et al., 1993; Van Den Oord et al., 1993).

Beside the relatively high stability and heritability of the Attention Problems syndrome per se, it also predicts a variety of later problems in addition to attention problems. For example, in path analyses that included all eight cross-informant syndromes and several other variables as candidate predictors, parent ratings of the Attention Problems syndrome significantly predicted not only attention problems, but also parent and teacher ratings of the Delinquent Behavior syndrome 3 years later (Stanger et al., 1992). Furthermore, the Attention Problems syndrome was the strongest 3-year predictor of a composite index of signs of disturbance, including suicidal behavior, referral for special education and mental health services, trouble with the police, and parents' judgment that help was needed for behavioral/ emotional problems (Stanger, Achenbach, & McConaughy, 1993). Even though the developmental stability and high heritability of the Attention Problems syndrome suggest trait-like qualities, the syndrome thus represents a risk factor for other kinds of problems, as well.

Research on the pre-1991 version of the CBCL Attention Problems syndrome has shown significant relations to diagnoses of Attention Deficit Disorder made from TRF ratings and clinical assessments (Barkley, DuPaul, & McMurray, 1990); to diagnoses from DISC-P interviews of parents (Edelbrock & Costello, 1988); and to diagnoses made from comprehensive clinical evaluations where the diagnoses were confirmed with the Diagnostic Interview for Children and Adolescents, Parent Version (DICA-P; Herjanic & Reich, 1982; Steingard, Biederman, Doyle, & Sprich-Buckminster, 1992). Adolescents meeting DSM-III-R criteria for ADHD have also been found to score significantly higher than control groups on the pre-1991 version of the TRF Attention Problems syndrome (Barkley, Anastopoulos, Guevremont, & Fletcher, 1991). Figure 6-2 depicts the percentage of children who qualified for ADD diagnoses within successive 5-point intervals of T scores on the syndrome scale scored from the CBCL. As can be seen in

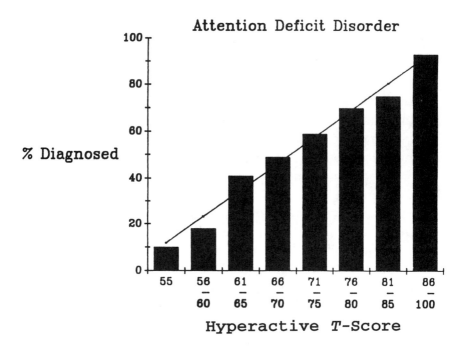

Figure 6-2. Relations between DSM-III diagnoses of Attention Deficit Disorder and scores on the pre-1991 CBCL Hyperactive scale.

Figure 6-2, there was a direct linear relation between syndrome scores and the probability of the diagnosis.

The Social Problems Syndrome

This syndrome has no clear counterparts in DSM-III, DSM-III-R, or DSM-IV. However, multivariate analyses have identified syndromes resembling it in at least 13 samples (Achenbach, 1992). The closest counterparts among the pre-1991 syndromes were designated as Unpopular on the TRF and YSR, Social Withdrawal for boys 6-11 on the CBCL, and Hostile Withdrawal for boys 12-16 on the CBCL. The pre-1991 counterparts correlated .78 to .98 with the 1991 Social Problems syndrome (Achenbach, 1991b, 1991c, 1991d). In comparisons of principal components derived from the ACQ Behavior Checklist and the American and Dutch CBCLs, a version was identified that was labeled Socially Inept (Achenbach, Conners, Quay, Verhulst, & Howell, 1989). Because there is no clear DSM counterpart for this syndrome and because the convergence of empirically derived versions on a unitary construct is relatively recent, less research has been published than on most of the other syndromes.

Despite the lack of recognition of this syndrome in the DSM, the heritability estimate of .65 for the CBCL Social Problems syndrome tied with Somatic Complaints for the highest heritability in the Edelbrock et al. (1993) twin study. The 3-year longitudinal stability r of the Social Problems syndrome was .50, which was among the four highest in the American national sample, although its 4-year stability r of .38 and 6-year stability r of .33 in the Dutch general population sample ranked somewhat lower within that sample (McConaughy et al., 1992; Verhulst & van der Ende, 1992).

In addition to the high heritability estimate obtained for Social Problems, the most notable finding to date is the exceptionally good cross-informant agreement in scores obtained from mothers, fathers, teachers, and youths. The higher agreement than for most other syndromes was evident in relative risk odds ratios computed for classification of children as deviant (T scores ≥ 67) by one type of informant in relation to classification of the children as deviant by each other type of informant. For YSR x TRF, YSR x CBCL, and TRF x CBCL agreement, the odds ratios ranged from 9.5 to 11.0, which were well above the odds ratios for any other syndromes scored from these combinations of instruments. For agreement between mothers and fathers on the CBCL, the odds ratio was 21.3, which was higher than the odds ratios for other pairs of informants, but lower than the very high mother x father odds ratios of 23.5 to 40.2 found for Attention Problems, Aggressive Behavior, and Delinquent Behavior (Achenbach, 1991a).

In an Australian sample of 362 11- to 16-year-olds, the Social Problems syndrome yielded higher agreement (mean $r = .62$) between parent-, teacher-, and self-ratings than any other syndrome. This degree of agreement between ratings by youths and their parents and teachers was especially striking, because the Social Problems syndrome comprises such items as *Acts too young for age, Too dependent, Doesn't get along with other kids, Gets teased a lot, Not liked by other kids, Poorly coordinated or clumsy,* and *Prefers being with younger kids,* which may be difficult for youths and even their parents to acknowledge (Sawyer, 1990; data presented by Achenbach, 1991c, 1991d). The Social Problems syndrome also yielded the second highest odds ratio for discrimination between referred and nonreferred children on the CBCL (odds ratio = 10.9) and TRF (odds ratio = 8.3; Achenbach, 1991b, 199c). The high heritability, high cross-informant agreement, and good discrimination between referred and nonreferred children all indicate that the Social Problems syndrome deserves far more attention than it has received.

The Thought Problems Syndrome

The pre-1991 syndromes that were most similar to the 1991 Thought Problems syndrome were designated as Schizoid for some sex/age groups on the CBCL, Obsessive-Compulsive for other groups on the CBCL and the TRF, and Thought Disorder on the YSR. The correlations between the 1991 Thought Problems syndrome and its pre-1991 counterparts ranged from .81 to .92. Syndromes resembling the Thought Problems syndrome have been identified in multivariate analyses of at least 22 samples (Achenbach, 1992). The CBCL Thought Problems syndrome has correlated .64 with the Psychotic scale of the Quay-Peterson (1983) Revised Behavior Problem Checklist (Achenbach, 1991b). The closest DSM counterpart to the Thought Problems syndrome is Schizotypal Personality Disorder, although the syndrome also shares some features of Obsessive-Compulsive Disorder and certain psychotic disorders. Because these are primarily adult diagnoses, there has been little research on their relations to the Thought Problems syndrome or its pre-1991 counterparts.

Most of the problems comprising the Thought Problems syndrome are reported for <10% of children in nonreferred samples scored on the CBCL and TRF. As a result, approximately 98% of nonreferred children obtain raw scores ≤4 on the CBCL and TRF Thought Problems scales. However, some items of the YSR Thought Problems scale are reported by more than half of nonreferred youths. An example is *Can't get mind off certain thoughts,* which is reported by close to 60% of nonreferred 15- to 18-year-olds (Achenbach, 1991d). Owing to the higher prevalence rates in self-reports, the 98th percentile raw score is 8 for boys and 9 for girls on the YSR Thought Problems scale, as compared to ≤4 on the CBCL and TRF Thought Problems scales.

A test-retest $r = .58$ has been obtained over a 7-month period for the YSR Thought Problems scale (Achenbach, 1991d). Parents' ratings yielded a stability $r = .30$ over 3 years in the American national sample (McConaughy et al., 1992), and .21 over 4 years and .17 over 6 years in the Dutch general population sample (Verhulst & van der Ende, 1992). Despite the low prevalence rate for Thought Problems items rated by parents, which may limit the stability of the scale, a significant heritability estimate of .47 was found in the Edelbrock et al. (1993) twin study. Although not among the strongest discriminators, the Thought Problems scale did discriminate significantly between referred and nonreferred samples on the CBCL, TRF, and YSR, according to multiple regression and odds ratio analyses (Achenbach, 1991b, 1991c, 1991d).

The resemblance of the Thought Problems syndrome to characteristics of schizotypal personality and schizophrenia suggest that it may be a precursor to disorders such as these that usually do not become evident until adulthood. Numerous studies have attempted to identify early precursors of later schizophrenia. In a study of children who met DSM-

III criteria for schizophrenia by age 10, CBCLs scored from case records showed elevated rates of problems on the pre-1991 versions of the Anxious/Depressed and Attention Problems syndromes, in addition to the criterial features of schizophrenia (Watkins, Asarnow, & Tanguay, 1988). However, no single pattern of early behavioral/emotional problems has been found to predict later schizophrenia with much certainty. Instead, it appears that a variety of behavioral/emotional problems, plus subtle deficits detectible on laboratory information processing tasks, may indicate elevated risks. Furthermore, the precursor behavioral/emotional problems may differ by sex, and other risk factors are also apt to be relevant (Nuechterlein, 1986).

The disorders that are currently diagnosed as schizophrenia probably involve a variety of complex causal factors (Gottesman, 1991). This heterogeneity and the difficulty of discriminating between those who truly do and do not have schizophrenia even in adulthood suggest that no single syndrome of childhood problems is likely to be a strong predictor of later schizophrenia. However, longitudinal research may be able to identify particular combinations of childhood syndromes with other factors that are related to relatively high versus low risk for schizophrenia-like problems at later developmental periods.

CORRELATES OF PROFILE TYPES

Because the profile types derived from the eight cross-informant syndromes are being introduced here for the first time, no other research on them has previously been published. The only findings to date are those that are reported here. Where relevant, however, findings on analogous profile types derived from pre-1991 CBCL syndromes will also be summarized.

To test relations between classification according to profile types and differences on other variables, we performed one-way analyses of covariance (ANCOVAs) in which children grouped according to profile type were compared on another variable that was treated as the dependent variable. As explained in Chapter 4, children were classified according to the profile type with which they had their highest ICC, if the ICC was ≥.445. Each one-way ANCOVA compared groups of children whose total problem scores were ≥30 and who were classified by each profile type that was applicable to their sex/age group on a particular instrument. For example, because CBCLs for 12-18-year-old boys can be classified according to seven profile types, each ANCOVA had seven cells. Each cell included boys whose profiles had ICCS ≥.445 with one of the four cross-informant profile types or one of the three CBCL-specific profile types that was scored for 12-18-year-old boys.

To prevent differences between profile types from being confounded with the overall degree of deviance, the total problem score was covaried out of the comparisons among profile types. If the overall F for the comparisons among profile types was significant at $p < .05$ after covarying out the total problem score, we computed least significant difference (LSD) contrasts between the scores obtained by children having each profile type versus every other type. If a contrast showed that children having a particular profile type differed significantly ($p ≤ .05$) from children having another profile type, this difference was considered to reflect a positive correlate of the profile type having the higher mean score and a negative correlate of the type having the lower mean score.

Separate ANCOVAs were done for children of each sex/age group on each instrument. The samples included referred and nonreferred children whose total problem raw scores were ≥30 on the instrument on which the profile types were scored. We will first summarize the correlates found most consistently for the four cross-informant profile types across the separate analyses of each sex/age group on the CBCL, TRF, and YSR. We will then summarize the correlates found for the instrument-specific profile types in each of the relevant data sets. We will not report every significant difference between profile types, but only the ways in which a particular profile type differed significantly from >1 other profile type in >1 sex/age group. In most cases, the differences reported were significant for several comparisons between one profile and other profiles in several sex/age groups.

Correlates of Cross-Informant Profile Types

Profiles Scored from the CBCL. Classification according-ing to types scored from the CBCL was tested for differences in the subjects' age within the 4-11 and 12-18-year ranges, ethnicity (white versus nonwhite), socioeconomic status (SES), scores on each competence scale and total competence, and all TRF scale scores. For testing the relation of CBCL profile types to demographic variables, the sample sizes ranged from 294 for girls 12-18 to 619 for boys 12-18. For testing the relations of CBCL profile types to TRF scores, the sample sizes ranged from 96 for girls 12-18 to 218 for boys 5-11.

The cross-informant profile types scored from the CBCL were not consistently related to age, ethnic, or SES differences among the children. However, in all four sex/age groups, children classified by the Withdrawn type obtained significantly higher (i.e., more favorable) scores on the CBCL School scale than did children classified by several other types. Children classified by the Withdrawn type scored from the CBCL also obtained significantly higher TRF Withdrawn and Internalizing scores and significantly lower TRF Delinquent, Aggressive, and Externalizing scores than did children classified by several other profile types.

The Somatic Complaints type scored from the CBCL had several correlates across multiple groups that were similar to those of the Withdrawn type, including high scores on the CBCL School and total competence scales and low scores on the TRF Delinquent, Aggressive, and Externalizing scales. However, children classified by the Somatic Complaints type also had relatively high scores on the CBCL competence scale designated as Social and the TRF Happy and total adaptive scales. They had relatively low scores on the TRF Withdrawn, Social Problems, Thought Problems, and Attention Problems scales.

Children classified by the CBCL Social Problems type differed from those classified by the Withdrawn and Somatic Complaints types in obtaining low scores on the CBCL Social, School, and total competence scales. The only TRF scale on which the Social Problems type showed significant differences from other types in several sex/age groups was the Happy scale, where the Social Problems type obtained relatively favorable scores.

The Delinquent-Aggressive type did not differ consistently from the other types on the CBCL competence scales. However, children classified according to the Delinquent-Aggressive type scored from the CBCL did differ significantly from other types on the following TRF scales: The Delinquent-Aggressive group obtained relatively low scores on the TRF total adaptive, Withdrawn, and Internalizing scales, but relatively high scores on the TRF Delinquent, Aggressive, and Externalizing scales.

As summarized in Table 6-1, all four types scored from the CBCL had some distinctive features, with the Withdrawn and Somatic Complaints types having the most features in common and the Delinquent-Aggressive type differing more markedly from the others. (The relatively small N of qualifying cases having the YSR precluded analyses of YSR correlates of the CBCL and TRF.)

In addition to testing correlates of profile types in terms of scale scores, we also tested their correlates in terms of signs of disturbance reported by parents in a national survey of 2,466 6- to 19-year-olds (Stanger, Achenbach, & McConaughy, 1993). The signs of disturbance reported by parents included special help for academic problems in school,

CORRELATES OF TAXA

Table 6-1
Consistent Correlates of Cross-Informant Profile Types

	Withdrawn		Somatic Complaints	
	High Scores	Low Scores	High Scores	Low Scores
CBCL Profile Types with CBCL Competence Scores				
	1. School	—	1. Social	—
	2. Total comp.		2. School	
			3. Total comp.	
CBCL Profile Types with TRF Scores				
	1. Withdrawn	1. Delinquent	1. Happy	1. Withdrawn
	2. Internalizing	2. Aggressive	2. Total adapt.	2. Social Prob.
		3. Externalizing		3. Thought Prob.
				4. Attention Prob.
				5. Delinquent
				6. Aggressive
				7. Externalizing
CBCL Profile Types with Signs of Disturbance				
	—	1. School behav. probs.	—	1. School behav. probs.
		2. Police contacts		2. Police contacts
		3. Total disturb.		3. Total disturb.
TRF Profile Types with TRF Adaptive Scores				
	—	1. Academic perf.	1. Academic perf.	—
		2. Happy	2. Working hard	
			3. Behaving approp.	
			4. Learning	
			5. Total adapt.	
TRF Profile Types with CBCL Scores				
	1. Withdrawn	1. Aggressive	1. School	1. Attention Prob.
	2. Internalizing	2. Externalizing		
YSR Profile Types with YSR Age & Competence Scores				
	1. Age	—	1. Academic perf.	—
	2. Academic perf.			
YSR Profile Types with Signs of Disturbance				
	—	1. Academic Probs.	—	1. Police contacts
		2. School behav. probs.		2. Total disturb.

Table 6-1 (cont.)

Social Problems		Delinquent-Aggressive	
High Scores	*Low Scores*	*High Scores*	*Low Scores*

CBCL Profile Types with CBCL Competence Scales			
—	1. Social	—	—
	2. School		
	3. Total comp.		
CBCL Profile Types with all TRF Scales			
1. Happy	—	1. Delinquent	1. Total adapt.
2. Internalizing		2. Aggressive	2. Withdrawn
		3. Externalizing	3. Internalizing
CBCL Profile Types with Signs of Disturbance			
1. School behav. probs.	1. Police contacts	1. School behav. probs.	—
2. Total disturb.		2. Police contacts	
		3. Total disturb.	

TRF Profile Types with TRF Adaptive			
1. Academic perf.	—	—	1. Behaving approp.
2. Total adapt.			2. Total adapt.
TRF Profile Types with all CBCL Scales			
—	1. Withdrawn	1. Aggressive	1. Withdrawn
		2. Externalizing	2. Attention Prob.
			3. Internalizing

YSR Profile Types with YSR Age & Competence Scales			
1. Academic perf.	—	1. Age	—
YSR Profile Types with Signs of Disturbance			
1. Academic probs.	1. School behav. probs.	1. Academic probs.	—
	2. Police contacts	2. School behav. probs.	
	3. Total disturb.	3. Police contacts	
		4. Total disturb.	

Note. Entries in the table indicate variables on which a profile type differed from >1 other profile type in >1 sex/age group at $p \leq .05$, according to least-significant-difference contrasts derived from 1-way ANCOVAs where total problem scores were covaried out.

serious behavior problems in school, police contacts related to the child's misbehavior, referral for mental health services, parents' judgment that the child needed additional help for behavioral/emotional problems, and the number of these signs reported for the child.

Because only a small proportion of the national sample was clinically deviant, children of all ages and both sexes were included in the same ANCOVA of each sign, if their total problem scores were ≥30 and they obtained significant ICCs with profile types. Only the profile types applicable to both sexes and all ages were included. These criteria yielded 353 6- to 19-year-olds for the ANCOVAs comparing the signs of disturbance reported for each profile type. As Table 6-1 shows, significantly fewer signs of disturbance were reported for the Withdrawn and Somatic Complaints types than for several other profile types. The Delinquent-Aggressive type had higher scores than other types on school behavior problems and total disturbance. The Social Problems type had relatively low scores for police contacts but high scores for school behavior problems and total disturbance.

Profiles Scored from the TRF. ANCOVAs were used to compare children classified according to TRF profile types with respect to differences on demographic variables, teachers' ratings on the TRF adaptive functioning scales, and parents' ratings on all CBCL scales. Sample sizes for the demographic variables and teachers' ratings of adaptive functioning ranged from 232 for 12- to 18-year-old girls to 700 for 5- to 11-year-old boys. For parents' CBCL ratings, sample sizes ranged from 60 for 12- to 18-year-old girls to 298 for 5- to 11-year-old boys. The availability of CBCLs for only 60 girls at ages 12-18 limited statistical power to detect significant CBCL correlates in this group.

As was also found for the CBCL profile types, children classified by the types scored from the TRF did not differ consistently with respect to ethnicity, SES or age within the

5 to 11 and 12 to 18 age ranges. However, the children who were classified by the TRF Withdrawn type tended to receive low scores from their teachers on the Academic and Happy scales. They also received relatively high scores from their parents on the CBCL Withdrawn scale and low scores on the Aggressive and Externalizing scales. The findings are summarized in Table 6-1.

Children classified by the Somatic Complaints type on the TRF received relatively high scores from their teachers on the Academic, Working Hard, Appropriately Behaving, Learning, and total adaptive scales. From their parents, they received relatively low scores on the CBCL Attention Problems scale.

Children who matched the TRF Social Problems type were distinguished from those who matched other types by relatively high scores on the Academic and total adaptive scales of the TRF. They also obtained relatively low scores from their parents on the CBCL Withdrawn and Delinquent scales.

The Delinquent-Aggressive type scored from the TRF identified children who obtained low TRF scores on the Appropriately Behaving and total adaptive scales. They also obtained low CBCL scores on the Withdrawn, Attention Problems, and Internalizing scales, but high scores on the Delinquent, Aggressive, and Externalizing scales. Because the TRF profile types had few significant associations with the signs of disturbance, these are not displayed in Table 6-1.

Profiles Scored from the YSR. Because too few subjects with YSR scores ≥ 30 had CBCLs or TRFs for meaningful comparisons among all profile types, only demographic variables, YSR competence scores, and signs of disturbance were tested as candidate correlates. The sample sizes were 364 for boys and 288 for girls. The ANCOVAs showed that youths who matched the Withdrawn and Delinquent-Aggressive types tended to be older than youths who matched the other types. Those who matched

the Withdrawn, Somatic Complaints, and Social Problems
types tended to report better academic performance than did
youths who matched the other types scored from the YSR.
Table 6-1 summarizes the correlates of the four cross-
informant syndrome types.

Table 6-1 also summarizes the signs of disturbance that
were significantly associated with the YSR versions of the
cross-informant profile types. As Table 6-1 shows, the
Withdrawn, Somatic Complaints, and Social Problems types
had relatively low scores on several signs of disturbance.
The Delinquent-Aggressive type, by contrast, had
significantly higher scores than most other groups on
academic problems, school behavior problems, police
contacts, and total disturbance. Thus, the picture of relatively
unmitigated conduct problems derived from the YSRs of
youths manifesting the Delinquent-Aggressive type was
borne out by the signs of disturbance independently reported
by their parents. The Delinquent-Aggressive type scored
from the CBCL showed similar associations with the signs
of disturbance.

Summary of Correlates of Cross-Informant Types

As shown in Table 6-1, children classified by either the
CBCL or TRF version of the Withdrawn type obtained
significantly lower scores than other children on Externalizing scales from both their parents and teachers. Children
classified by the CBCL and YSR versions of the Withdrawn
type also had relatively few signs of disturbance.
Furthermore, those who were classified by the Withdrawn
type by parents received high scores on the Withdrawn scale
from teachers. There was a contradiction, however, between
the relatively low TRF scores for academic performance
obtained by children classified on the TRF as Withdrawn and
the relatively high CBCL scores for School and YSR scores
for academic performance obtained by children classified as
Withdrawn on these instruments. Whereas the TRF and YSR

scores only include current academic performance, the CBCL scale also includes special class placement, repeating grades, and other school problems. The differences in scale composition might partly explain the difference between the CBCL and TRF findings. However, the inconsistency between the findings for TRF and YSR academic performance scores may be explained by the fact that teachers would be identifying only the most extremely withdrawn children, as they would not usually view less withdrawn children as needing special help.

For children classified according to the Somatic Complaints type, parent-, teacher-, and self-reports were generally consistent in showing relatively high scores for competence and adaptive functioning, including academic performance. Parents' and teachers' ratings were also consistent in yielding low scores on the Attention Problems syndrome, although teachers' ratings of children classified by the CBCL Somatic Complaints type yielded low scores for five additional syndromes, as well. Children manifesting the Somatic Complaints profile type on the CBCL are thus seen by their teachers as having relatively few behavioral/emotional problems in most areas of school functioning. Children classified by the CBCL and YSR Somatic Complaints type also had relatively few signs of disturbance.

Children classified by the Social Problems type presented a mixed picture of low competence as seen by their parents but somewhat better adaptive functioning as seen by their teachers, and good academic performance according to their self-reports on the YSR. Although children classified by the TRF Social Problems type received relatively low scores on the CBCL Withdrawn and Delinquent Behavior syndromes, other problem scales did not consistently differentiate this group from other profile types. Children classified by the CBCL and YSR Social Problems type were similar in having few police contacts but differed somewhat on other signs of disturbance.

As can be seen from Table 6-1, there was considerable consistency between teachers' ratings of problem scales for children classified according to the Delinquent-Aggressive profile type from the CBCL and vice versa for parents' ratings of children classified from the TRF. Such children were clearly seen as high on externalizing problems and low on internalizing problems by both types of informants. Several signs of disturbance indicative of externalizing problems were also significantly associated with the Delinquent-Aggressive type scored from the YSR, as well as from the CBCL.

In summary, our initial analyses of the cross-informant profile types have revealed numerous significant differences between the types in problem and adaptive scores obtained from different kinds of informants than those on whose ratings the profile classifications were made. The absence of consistent demographic differences indicates that the profile types and their correlates reflect perceptions of behavioral/emotional patterns per se rather than perceptions of differences related to the age, ethnicity, or SES of the children.

Correlates of Profile Types Specific to Each Instrument

Types Specific to the CBCL. The three profile types specific to the CBCL were designated as *Social Problems-Attention Problems, Withdrawn-Anxious/Depressed-Aggressive* (boys only), and *Delinquent*. In the ANCOVAs that included these three profile types with the four cross-informant profile types scored from the CBCL, the only significant correlate of the Withdrawn-Anxious/Depressed-Aggressive type was that boys who matched it were significantly older than boys who matched three other types within both the 4-11 and 12-18 age range, as indicated in Table 6-2. Conversely, among 4- to 11-year-old boys and girls, those who matched the Delinquent type were significantly younger than those who matched two other profile types. Children who matched the

CBCL Delinquent type also received low scores on the CBCL School and total competence scales, as well as on the TRF Happy and total adaptive scales. They received relatively high scores on the TRF Delinquent, Aggressive, and Externalizing scales. They also scored high on school behavior problems, police contacts, and total disturbance.

Children classified by the Social Problems-Attention Problems profile type received low scores on the CBCL Social, School, and total competence scales. They received relatively high scores on the TRF Withdrawn and Social Problems scales.

Types Specific to the TRF. Of the two types specific to the TRF, the type designated as *Attention Problems* had considerably more correlates than the type designated as *Withdrawn-Thought Problems*, as Table 6-2 shows. Among 5- to 11-year-olds of both sexes, those matching the Attention Problems type were significantly younger than those matching all the other types. On the TRF, they also obtained significantly lower scores than most other profile types for Academic Performance, Working Hard, Behaving Appropriately, and total adaptive functioning. Yet, they also obtained significantly higher scores than several other groups for Happy. This suggests that these children may be blissfully unaware of the problems that others perceive in their behavior. On the CBCL, their parents gave them relatively low scores on the Withdrawn scale and high scores on the Attention Problems and Aggressive Behavior scales.

Children who matched the TRF Withdrawn-Thought Problems type obtained high scores on the CBCL Withdrawn scale and low scores on the Aggressive scale, but otherwise did not differ consistently from children who matched the other TRF profile types.

Types Specific to the YSR. The three types specific to the YSR were designated as *YSR Social Problems, Attention Problems-Delinquent-Aggressive* (boys only), and *Delinquent*

Table 6-2
Consistent Correlates of Instrument-Specific Profile Types

	Withdrawn-Anx/Dep-Aggressive[a]		CBCL Types Social Probs.-Attention Probs.[b]		Delinquent	
	High Scores	Low Scores	High Scores	Low Scores	High Scores	Low Scores
CBCL Profile Types with Age and CBCL Competence Scores						
	1. Age	—	—	1. Social 2. School 3. Total comp.	—	1. Age 2. School 3. Total comp.
CBCL Profile Types with TRF Scores						
	—	—	1. Withdrawn 2. Social Probs.	—	1. Delinquent 2. Aggressive 3. Externalizing	1. Happy 2. Total adapt.
CBCL Profile Types with Signs of Disturbance						
Age/sex-specific types were not tested.					1. School behav. probs. 2. Police contacts 3. Total disturb.	—

Note. Entries in the table indicate variables on which a profile type differed from >1 other profile type in >1 sex/age group at $p \leq .05$, according to least-significant-difference contrasts derived from 1-way ANCOVAs where total problem scores were covaried out.

TRF Types

	Withdrawn-Thought Problems[c]		Attention Problems	
	High Scores	**Low Scores**	**High Scores**	**Low Scores**
TRF Profile Types with Age & TRF Adaptive Scores		—	1. Happy	1. Age 2. Academic perf. 3. Working hard 4. Behaving approp. 5. Total adapt.
TRF Profile Types with CBCL Scores	1. Withdrawn	1. Aggressive	1. Attention Probs.	1. School 2. Withdrawn

YSR Types

	YSR Social Problems		Attention Probs.-Del.-Aggress.[a]	Delinquent[d]
	High Scores	**Low Scores**		
YSR Types with Signs of Disturbance	—	1. Academic Probs. 2. School behav. Probs. 3. Police contacts 4. Total disturb.	Sex-specific types were not tested.	

[a]Boys only [b]Ages 12-18 only [c]Ages 5-11 only [d]Girls only

(girls only). The only significant demographic correlate found for these types was the tendency for youths who matched the YSR Social Problems type to be younger than those who matched the other YSR types. However, as Table 6-2 shows, the YSR Social Problems type that was common to both sexes had significantly lower scores than other profile types on academic problems, school behavior problems, police contacts, and total disturbance. According to these specific signs of disturbance reported by parents, youths who reported problems corresponding to the YSR Social Problems type had fewer overt problems than youths' classified by the other YSR profile types.

CORRELATES OF PRE-1993 PROFILE TYPES

Several studies have tested relations between the pre-1993 versions of the CBCL profile types and other variables. (There were no pre-1993 profile types for the TRF or YSR.) In the study that derived the pre-1993 CBCL profile types for ages 6-11 and 12-16, the profile types showed numerous significant differences with respect to demographic variables and the CBCL competence scales (Edelbrock & Achenbach, 1980). Similar analyses were done when CBCL profile types were derived for ages 4 and 5 (Achenbach & Edelbrock, 1983). Findings for the 1993 profiles resemble some of the findings for the earlier profile types. However, the use of the same eight cross-informant syndromes for all sex/age groups, the derivation of core profile types whenever possible for all sex-age groups on a particular instrument, and the focus on profile types that had counterparts across instruments all contribute to differences between the 1993 and earlier types. These differences, in turn, lead to differences in their associations with other variables.

In an extensive test of the correlates of the pre-1991 profile types, 6-11-year-old referred boys classified by each type were compared with respect to CBCL competence scales, all TRF scales, scores on the Direct Observation

Form (DOF; see Achenbach, 1991b), the Wechsler Intelligence Scale for Children-Revised (WISC-R; Wechsler, 1974), the Peabody Individual Achievement Test (PIAT; Dunn & Markwardt, 1970), and several personality measures (McConaughy, Achenbach, & Gent, 1988).

Classification of boys according to the profile types was significantly related to all classes of variables that were tested, with some parallels to our current findings. For example, boys who matched the pre-1993 Somatic Complaints type obtained relatively high scores for CBCL total competence and TRF adaptive functioning, as we also found for children classified by the 1993 Somatic Complaints profile types. Conversely, boys classified by the pre-1993 Delinquent type obtained relatively low TRF adaptive functioning scores and high TRF Aggressive and Externalizing scores, as we also found for children classified by the 1993 Delinquent-Aggressive type. Although we have not yet tested relations between the 1993 profile types and measures of ability or achievement, the pre-1993 counterpart of the Withdrawn-Anxious/Depressed-Aggressive type was remarkable for being associated with higher WISC-R IQs and PIAT scores than all the other profile types in the sample of 6-11-year-old boys, despite also having higher CBCL total problem scores than any other profile type in that sample.

Other studies of the pre-1993 profile types have reported significantly better functioning for children classified by profile types reflecting primarily internalizing characteristics than for children having primarily externalizing profiles. The better functioning was documented via the TRF (McArdle & Mattison, 1989), IQ and reading tests, measures of coping, school behavior problems, and observance of school rules (Cohen, Gotlieb, Kershner, & Wehrspann, 1985). The pre-1993 profile types were also found to discriminate significantly between children independently diagnosed as meeting DSM-III criteria for Overanxious Disorder and ADDH (Mattison & Bagnato, 1987). Although the findings on the pre-1993 profile types cannot be applied directly to the 1993 types, they do indicate that profile types derived by our cluster analytic methodology have important external correlates.

SUMMARY

This chapter presented a sampling of correlates found for the eight cross-informant syndromes and their predecessors. The combination of anxiety and depression reflected in the *Anxious/Depressed* syndrome corresponds to the construct of *negative affectivity* that has been proposed to explain the co-occurrence of diverse forms of dysphoric affect. According to the construct of negative affectivity, some people have a disposition to experience dysphoric affect across diverse situations even in the absence of overt stress. The Anxious/Depressed syndrome has been found to discriminate significantly between children diagnosed as having affective disorders and those not having such disorders based on diagnoses made from case histories, structured psychiatric interviews with parents, and structured and semistructured interviews with the children themselves. The hypothesis that depressed mothers' CBCL ratings exaggerate their children's psychopathology has not been supported.

In the DSM nosology, the closest analog to the *Withdrawn* syndrome is Avoidant Disorder, which has received little attention. Despite the lack of attention to its nosological counterpart, the Withdrawn syndrome discriminates strongly between referred and nonreferred children in parent-, teacher-, and self-ratings. It has yielded a heritability estimate of .59 and may work against the development of aggressive behavior in some children.

The *Somatic Complaints* syndrome resembles the DSM Somatization Disorder, although DSM does not acknowledge its existence in preadolescents. A heritability estimate of .65 has been obtained for the Somatic Complaints syndrome, and it has been significantly associated with other measures of somatic problems that have no detectible organic causes.

Although the DSM nosology combines aggressive and delinquent behaviors in the diagnosis of Conduct Disorder, there is considerable evidence for their separability into two syndromes that are moderately but far from perfectly correlated with each other. The *Aggressive Behavior* syndrome has yielded higher heritability estimates and greater long-term stabilities than the *Delinquent Behavior* syndrome. High correlations have been found between the Aggressive syndrome and biomedical measures indicative of low serotonergic activity. There is considerable evidence that the Aggressive syndrome is affected more by biological factors than the Delinquent syndrome, which appears to primarily reflect behavior learned by biologically normal individuals.

The *Attention Problems* syndrome has shown high long-term stability and predictive relations to a variety of later problems. It has yielded a heritability estimate of .64 and strong associations with diagnoses of attention deficit disorders according to various external criteria.

The *Social Problems* syndrome has no clear counterpart in the DSM nosology. Nevertheless, it yielded a heritability estimate of .65, strong discrimination between referred and nonreferred children, and exceptionally high cross-informant agreement among mothers, fathers, teachers, and even youths, despite its inclusion of several items that would seem difficult for parents and youths to report.

The *Thought Problems* syndrome consists of items having low prevalence in parent- and teacher-reports, but some of its items are reported by more than half of non-referred youths. It resembles the DSM categories of Schizotypal Personality and Schizophrenia, although evidence to date indicates that childhood precursors of schizophrenia are diverse, including problems of the Anxious/Depressed and Attention Problems syndromes. Despite the low prevalence rates of its items, the CBCL Thought Problems syndrome has yielded a significant heritability of .47.

Because the cross-informant profile types are being introduced with this book, there has been no previous research on them. Comparisons of children classified by these and by the instrument-specific types have shown numerous within- and cross-informant differences on the competence and problem scales of the CBCL and TRF, as well as on separate reports of signs of disturbance, as summarized in Tables 6-1 and 6-2. Pre-1993 versions of the profile types have also yielded significant associations with a variety of measures.

Chapter 7
Using Empirically Based
Syndromes and Profile Types

Chapter 6 presented a sampling of empirical correlates and theoretical implications of the syndromes and profile types derived from the CBCL, TRF, and YSR. The findings summarized in Chapter 6 reflect only a few applications of the CBCL, TRF, and YSR. References for many other applications can be found in the *Bibliography of Published Studies Using the Child Behavior Checklist and Related Materials* (Brown & Achenbach, 1993), which lists publications according to over 200 topics and is updated annually.

The CBCL, TRF, and YSR Manuals illustrate applications of each of the three instruments, while the *Integrative Guide* (Achenbach, 1991a) illustrates ways of coordinating the cross-informant syndromes in practical and research applications. The present chapter outlines research and practical applications that capitalize on the additional options provided by the profile types. The profile types do not replace the syndromes, but supplement them by providing an additional basis for identifying similarities and differences among children. For some purposes, grouping children according to deviance on a particular syndrome and considering the correlates of that syndrome may be highly informative.

As an example, the findings reviewed in Chapter 6 indicate significant correlates and heritability for the Somatic Complaints syndrome. Furthermore, this syndrome has relatively low correlations with the other seven cross-informant syndromes in parent-, teacher-, and self-reports (Achenbach, 1991b, 1991c, 1991d). The Somatic Complaints syndrome also has the lowest comorbidity rate with deviant scores on the other syndromes (McConaughy & Achenbach, 1993). High scores on the Somatic Complaints syndrome thus tend to occur among children who do not have high scores on other syndromes and the scores tend to have fairly uncomplicated relations to other variables. In addition, our cluster analyses have identified a profile pattern that includes high scores on the Somatic Complaints syndrome and relatively low scores on the other seven syndromes. A similar profile pattern was identified in the pre-1993 cluster analyses of the CBCL for most sex/age groups on the CBCL (Achenbach & Edelbrock, 1983).

The profile type designated as Somatic Complaints may be useful in distinguishing children who are deviant only on Somatic Complaints from children who are deviant on other syndromes as well. The profile type can thus help to identify children whose problems are concentrated most exclusively in the Somatic Complaints syndrome. Although classification based only on the Somatic Complaints syndrome would usually be fairly concordant with classification based on the profile type, the degree of concordance would be affected by several factors. These include the cutpoints chosen for the syndrome scores and how children's scores on syndromes other than Somatic Complaints contribute to the ICC between their profiles and the Somatic Complaints profile type, and whether the children's total problem scores were ≥ 30 (the minimum required for computing ICCs with profile types).

The Somatic Complaints profile type is relatively low on all other scales, and the Somatic Complaints syndrome has relatively low comorbidity with other syndromes (McConaughy & Achenbach, 1993). Concordance between classification according to the Somatic Complaints type and the syndrome is thus likely to be higher than concordance between other types and syndromes. As an example, the Anxious/Depressed syndrome reflects problems that are certainly important in their own right. However, this syndrome has relatively high correlations and high comorbidity with certain other syndromes (Achenbach, 1991b, 1991c, 1991d; McConaughy & Achenbach, 1993). Furthermore, no profile type was identified that is elevated only on the Anxious/Depressed syndrome while being low on all other syndromes. In addition, considerable research suggests that problems like those comprising the Anxious/Depressed syndrome may reflect a broad disposition to negative affectivity (Finch et al., 1989; Watson & Clark, 1984).

Negative affectivity may often be associated with a wide variety of other problems. As a result, classification of children according to the Anxious/Depressed syndrome is apt to be less concordant with classification according to profile types than is classification according to the Somatic Complaints syndrome. In fact, the lack of a clearcut profile type that is elevated mainly on the Anxious/Depressed syndrome and the high comorbidity of this syndrome with other syndromes argue against classifying children only on the basis of the Anxious/Depressed syndrome in isolation from other syndromes. Because children who are elevated on this syndrome are likely to differ widely with respect to other problems, it is especially important to consider the entire profile and the ICCs with all profile types when focusing on the Anxious/Depressed syndrome. Additional syndromes whose high comorbidity rates affect relations between syndrome- and profile-based taxonomies include Aggressive Behavior and Attention Problems, as discussed in later sections.

RESEARCH USE OF SYNDROMES AND PROFILE TYPES

Research seeks to establish generalizable knowledge that can be tested and applied in multiple situations. One goal of establishing such knowledge is to apply it to helping individual children, each of whom is in many respects unique. Although research-based knowledge cannot encompass every idiosyncrasy of each individual case, research is the means by which important similarities and differences are detected. After the important similarities and differences are detected, knowledge gained from research cases can be applied to other cases. By linking new cases to taxonomically similar cases from which knowledge has been accumulated, we are able to make use of previously identified consistencies in behaviors when evaluating and treating the new cases. As stated by Messick (1989), the objective "is not to explain any single isolated event, behavior, or item response," but "to account for *consistency* in behaviors or item responses " (p. 14).

Bootstrapping Research

It has been repeatedly emphasized that there is unlikely to be any single correct approach or any single gold standard for judging the value of a particular approach. Instead, if we acknowledge that no one really knows the true boundaries between most childhood disorders, it is clear that research must pursue a "bootstrapping" strategy. That is, we must "lift ourselves by our own bootstraps." This entails *(1)* developing admittedly imperfect procedures for assessing and grouping variables that are themselves imperfectly defined; *(2)* testing the correlates of the imperfect assessment and taxonomic procedures; *(3)* using the findings to improve the procedures and our concepts of the variables that they assess; and *(4)* repeating this process to further improve and broaden the procedures and the hypothesized variables.

If the assessment procedures are psychometrically sound and yield important correlates, they can begin to serve as validating criteria for other procedures and hypothesized variables. As Cronbach and Meehl (1955) pointed out long ago, our confidence in particular hypothesized variables (*hypothetical constructs*) increases as *nomological* (lawful) networks of relations to other variables are supported.

Because neither our assessment procedures nor our hypothesized variables are expected to be error-free, their worth cannot be judged on the basis of a single study. Instead, they should be judged in terms of their cumulative contribution to empirically based knowledge.

Not all important research tasks can be accomplished at once. In fact, many research tasks cannot be accomplished at all until variables have been adequately defined and practical procedures are available for assessing them. Research tasks therefore need to be prioritized in order to start with tasks that are prerequisites for other tasks. However, most fundamental research tasks cannot be accomplished in complete isolation from one another. Instead, according to the bootstrapping strategy, an iterative sequence is required to move from imperfect definition and assessment of variables, to the identification of correlates, followed by improvements in definitions and assessment in order to strengthen associations with important correlates.

To advance empirically based taxonomy of child psychopathology, the bootstrapping process requires standardized assessment procedures, repeated testing of the assessment procedures to ensure that they are reliable and practical, and aggregation of the assessment data to form taxonomic groupings. To ensure that the criterial features of the taxonomic groupings discriminate between deviant and nondeviant criterion groups, it is also necessary to do epidemiological research on normative samples of the relevant populations, to compare the distributions of criterial features in normative and clinical samples, and to construct criteria for judging the degree of deviance manifested by individual children.

This bootstrapping strategy has already yielded reliably scorable syndromes that have been normed on large representative samples and have been found to have numerous correlates. Following iterative testing of numerous pilot editions of the CBCL, TRF, and YSR, derivation of syndromes went through two major iterations. The most recent iteration (Achenbach, 1991a) highlighted the common elements of syndromes for children of both sexes and different ages, rated by different informants. The derivation of profile types has also gone through two major iterations. The initial iteration involved only the CBCL (Achenbach & Edelbrock 1983; Edelbrock & Achenbach, 1980). However, the 1993 iteration involved profile types common to the CBCL, TRF, and YSR, plus types specific to each of these instruments. Now that profile types are available for all three instruments, their meaning and value can be tested with procedures similar to those used to test the syndromes, as outlined in the following sections.

Longitudinal Research

Although there has already been extensive bootstrapping research, much remains to be done to test the developmental course of the syndromes and profile types, as well as to test their relations to other important variables. The developmental findings may lead to further modifications of the empirically based taxa. Longitudinal research has already shown differences in the stabilities and predictive power of different syndromes (e.g., McConaughy et al., 1992; Stanger et al., 1992; Stanger, Achenbach, & McConaughy, 1993; Verhulst & van der Ende, 1992). Furthermore, upward extensions of the CBCL and YSR have been developed for tracing the same kinds of problems, syndromes, and profile types into adulthood (Achenbach, 1990a, 1990b). The adult versions of the CBCL and YSR are being used in longitudinal studies testing the prediction of adult problems and syndromes from scores obtained in childhood and adolescence. Adult outcomes are being assessed both in terms of empirically based taxonomy and in terms of DSM diagnoses.

Relations to DSM

Although the DSM shapes much of the research that is done on both child and adult psychopathology, it is important to avoid restricting research to the DSM categories. These categories have undergone many changes from DSM-III to DSM-III-R and DSM-IV. Furthermore, the DSM categories are not empirically based and have not been firmly validated. It would therefore not be surprising if the actual patterns of child and adult problems and the developmental relations between them do not conform to the DSM categories.

To properly test any correlates of DSM diagnoses, it is essential that the diagnoses be made on the basis of appropriate data and that good reliability be demonstrated for the diagnoses. The DSM does not operationally define its diagnostic categories in terms of specific assessment procedures. Furthermore, diagnoses made from interviews with children often disagree with those made from other data, such as parent- and teacher-reports (e.g., Bird, Gould, & Staghezza, 1992). Any test of DSM diagnoses requires a choice of assessment operations (e.g., particular clinical interviews), applied to particular sources of data (e.g., children, parents, teachers), and yielding multisource data combined in rigorous ways. Because no single procedure has been well validated for accomplishing these tasks, different threats to the reliability and validity of DSM diagnoses can arise in relation to any combination of procedures chosen for a particular study. The use of data from sources inappropriate for testing particular correlates, or combined inappropriately, or yielding unreliable diagnoses will necessarily limit the magnitude of associations between the DSM diagnoses and other variables, such as empirically based taxa.

If reliable DSM diagnoses are made from appropriate data, research that employs both DSM and empirically based taxonomies can illuminate both the points of contact between them and the areas in which only one of the two systems identifies important patterns of problems. As illustrated in Chapter 6, for example, the Withdrawn and Social Problems syndromes discriminate well between referred and nonreferred children and have other important correlates. Yet, they have no clearcut counterparts in the DSM. Research employing only DSM categories would thus miss these potentially important patterns of problems. Furthermore, the profile types provide taxonomic groupings based on higher order patterns of syndromes that may be more informative than groupings based on syndromes or diagnostic categories taken one-by-one.

Chapter 6 summarized several studies that reported significant concurrent relations between DSM-III diagnoses and the empirically based taxa (e.g., Edelbrock & Costello, 1988; Mattison & Bagnato, 1987; Rey & Morris-Yates, 1992; Weinstein et al., 1990). However, research is needed to test relations between empirically based taxa and the DSM-IV versions of the diagnostic categories. Furthermore, it would be desirable to compare the longitudinal course of disorders defined according to DSM-IV criteria with the longitudinal course of disorders scored according to the empirically based taxa. Such research could compare the DSM and empirically based systems with respect to the long-term stability and change found for disorders, as each system defines them. Such research could also reveal the degree to which the criteria used by each system successfully predict good versus poor outcomes and their accuracy in predicting particular types of outcomes, such as adult diagnoses.

Because the DSM and empirically based systems use somewhat different data and aggregate the data differently, it would also be valuable to test various combinations of the two systems as predictors of outcomes. In doing so, it would be worth testing the combined predictive power of classification according to profile types, scores on individual syndromes, and DSM diagnoses. This could be done by using multivariate statistics, such as discriminant analyses, to find the best combination of predictors for particular kinds of outcomes. Such analyses might show, for example, that a particular combination of childhood *profile types* and DSM diagnoses provided the most accurate predictions of adult antisocial behavior. On the other hand, a particular combination of *syndrome* scores and other DSM diagnoses might more accurately predict adult depression.

Such findings could advance taxonomic bootstrapping by improving the mix of data to be used for constructing taxonomies that have strong long-term correlates. The findings could also be used to construct models for the developmental course of different disorders. For example, the taxonomic features that predict poor versus good outcomes of various kinds may mark specific risk and protective factors that will help to illuminate the underlying developmental sequences. This has implications both for making decisions about particular cases and for intervention research, as addressed next.

IMPROVING DECISION-MAKING

One of the primary tasks of mental health professionals is to assess people who have behavioral/emotional problems. A second primary task is to make decisions about how best to help people who have problems. For example, if a concerned mother calls a clinic about her child's behavior, a decision must initially be made about whether the mother's report indicates a severe enough problem to warrant clinical evaluation. It must also be decided whether the clinic is the most appropriate place for evaluating the problem or whether the family should be referred elsewhere. If it is decided that the problem should be evaluated at the clinic, numerous additional decisions will be needed, such as the following:

1. What assessment data should be obtained from what sources?

2. How should the data be combined?

3. Are the child's problems severe enough to warrant intervention?

4. If so, what interventions would be optimal?

5. How much will the interventions improve the child's outcome?

6. If an intervention is begun, how long should it continue?

7. If the child does not improve, what should be done next?

Our ability to deal with questions such as these can be improved by using empirically based taxa both in research and in practical decision-making. The following sections outline a framework for interfacing research with the kinds of decisions required of those who work with troubled children. The overall framework may seem Utopian, but it can be helpful in highlighting relations among different problems and tasks that might otherwise seem haphazard and unrelated.

Clinical Decision-Making

In most clinical settings, Questions 1-7 are decided by clinicians on the basis of their past experience and their views of the particular case, plus factors extraneous to the case itself, such as the clinic's treatment philosophy, availability of particular therapists, financial considerations, etc. Leaving aside the extraneous factors, most decisions would be based primarily on the clinician's mental representation of the case at the point in time when the decision is required. This representation is likely to be affected by the clinician's previous experience, the clinician's matching of the case to memories of previous cases, and the clinician's judgment of what would be best for the client. Decision-making on the basis of mental processing of information in this fashion is called the *clinical* or *case-study method* (Dawes, Faust, & Meehl, 1989).

Actuarial Decision-Making

In contrast to the clinical method, the *actuarial* or *statistical method* bases decisions on explicit rules for applying previous empirical findings to individual cases (Dawes et al., 1989). Both the clinical and actuarial approaches to decision-making can use similar sorts of data, such as test scores, ratings of behavioral/emotional problems, developmental histories, and demographics. Both approaches can also use automation to produce conclusions from certain data. For example, "expert systems" computer programs automate the clinical method by making the same responses to particular data as expert clinicians would. Unlike the clinical method, however, the actuarial method applies decision rules that reflect the actual relations between assessment data and the outcomes found in previous cases.

Actuarial Models. A classic model for the actuarial method is the system used by insurance companies to set life insurance premiums. Data are continually collected on death rates in the general population. Actuarial tables are then constructed for people according to age and other factors that are found to be associated with death rates. Premiums for particular classes of people (e.g., 35-year-old physicians) are computed on the basis of the death rates found for large numbers of people having those characteristics. Thus, when 35-year-old Dr. Fuller applies for life insurance, the actuarial method decides the premium according to the death rate found in preceding years for 35-year-old people who are similar to Dr. Fuller with respect to variables related to death rate.

If the clinical method were used to set premiums, the insurance agent (or perhaps an expert system computer program) would decide Dr. Fuller's premium on the basis of a judgment about when Dr. Fuller is likely to die. The crucial difference is that the actuarial method uses data about applicants to assign them to a class for which the death rate is known. The decision about Dr. Fuller is then based on the known death rate for that class of people, rather than on a prediction that is specific to Dr. Fuller. As long as the death rate for new insurees is similar to the death rate for people whose data determined the premiums, the insurance company can properly cover Dr. Fuller and others, without having to decide precisely when each individual will die.

The actuarial method is not restricted to classification of people according to categorical outcomes such as death in relation to obvious demographic characteristics such as age and occupation. Many applications of the actuarial method employ quantitative assessment data to predict outcomes that are also quantified. An example is the use of high school grade point average (GPA) and college entrance exam scores to predict college GPA. College admissions officers use multiple regression equations to compute the actual relations of high school GPA and exam scores to college GPA among students already attending their colleges. The weights obtained for high school GPA and exam scores are then applied to the prediction of college GPAs for applicants in subsequent years.

The predictive relations can be used quantitatively to identify those applicants who are most desirable because their GPAs are the highest. The admissions officers can also use the actuarial prediction of college GPA in a categorical fashion by accepting only those students whose high school GPAs and exam scores predict passing GPAs in college.

Numerous studies have compared clinical and actuarial methods of decision-making in many fields. Examples include using Minnesota Multiphasic Personality Inventory (MMPI) profiles to distinguish between neurotic and psychotic psychiatric patients; using cognitive testing to diagnose progressive brain dysfunction; and predicting parole violations among candidates for parole from prison. According to a review by Dawes et al. (1989), virtually all direct comparisons have shown that the actuarial method equaled or exceeded the clinical method in achieving agreement with independent external criteria. Even where the assessment data were ratings of clinical judgments, the actuarial method of basing decisions on empirically obtained relations between the ratings and external criteria proved superior to the clinical method whereby clinicians base predictions about individuals on their own judgments.

In an example cited by Dawes et al., pathologists made predictions of patients' survival time following initial diagnoses of Hodgkin's disease by means of biopsy. (The study was done before Hodgkin's disease was controllable.) The assessment data consisted of the pathologists' ratings of the biopsy slides along nine dimensions that they identified as relevant. In a test of the clinical method, the pathologists' own predictions about individual patients showed virtually no relation to the patients' actual survival time. However, actuarial formulas were also computed for the relations between the pathologists' ratings and survival time in 100 cases. When tested on the next 93 cases, the actuarial formulas showed significant relations to the patients' survival time. Thus, even when the assessment data were subjective ratings by pathologists, the actuarial method made more accurate predictions than did the pathologists when they mentally processed their own judgments.

Advantages of Actuarial Decision-Making

Many factors interfere with making valid decisions from complex data. Several well documented biases in mental processing of information may be especially troublesome in judgments of child psychopathology (reviewed and illustrated by Achenbach, 1985). It is exceedingly difficult to keep track of the diverse and sometimes contradictory data from multiple sources relevant to decisions about children's problems, much less to appropriately weight each bit of data and combine the data in a consistent fashion.

A key source of the actuarial method's superiority is its greater consistency in using particular assessment data in the same way from case to case, according to the previously identified relations between the assessment data and outcomes. Even the most expert human judges are apt to use data inconsistently from one case to another, owing to factors such as the order in which the data are considered, fatigue, distractions, and idiosyncratic mental associations to each case. Furthermore, a clinician's personal experience encompasses a much smaller and less representative sample of cases than can be incorporated into actuarial systems that draw on cases seen by many clinicians.

Applying an Actuarial Strategy to Child Mental Health Services

The CBCL, TRF, YSR, and related instruments can be used to obtain data in a consistent fashion from case to case. Their empirically based aggregation of problem items into syndrome scales and profile types provides foci for accumulating actuarial data from which to derive decision rules for improving child mental health services. For example, if we apply an actuarial strategy to the seven questions listed earlier, we may be able to make better use of data that are currently available for making decisions about individual cases. This strategy will also facilitate research to improve our ways of helping children. Table 7-1 outlines an actuarial strategy for answering the seven questions. The following sections discuss Questions 1 through 7.

1. Assessment Data. To answer Question 1 in Table 7-1, an actuarial approach would start with assessment data that

Table 7-1
An Actuarial Strategy for Answering Clinical Questions

---

1. What assessment data should be obtained from what sources?
Answer: Construct assessment data base from which to predict outcomes: e.g., CBCL, demographics, developmental history, family composition; TRF for children attending school; YSR from 11-18-year-olds; SCIC from clinician; ability & achievement scores from tests; medical data from physician; DSM diagnoses, Axis IV Psychosocial Stressor score, Axis V Global Assessment of Functioning score.

2. How should the assessment data be combined?
Answer: Test various methods of combining data to maximize relations to important outcome variables.

3. Are the problems severe enough to warrant intervention?
Answer: Use clinical cutpoints to identify deviance on CBCL, TRF, & YSR scales; combine CBCL, TRF, YSR, & other assessment data to test outcomes with & without intervention; identify predictors of poor outcomes without intervention vs. better outcomes with intervention.

4. If intervention is warranted, what would be optimal?
Answer: Compare the effects of different interventions on children grouped according to profile type & other assessment data to identify interventions that are effective for particular groups of children.

5. How much will interventions improve outcomes?
Answer: In testing interventions, compute the *magnitude* of significant effects and the degree to which they achieve normal functioning. Interventions that produce small effects at great cost or risk may not be good options.

6. If an intervention is begun, how long should it continue?
Answer: Tests of interventions should be designed to determine how long they take to yield optimal results. These findings can be used to estimate the length of interventions in individual cases.

7. If the child does not improve, what should be done next?
Answer: Do periodic reassessments to determine whether the desired changes are occurring, e.g., by readministering the CBCL, TRF, YSR. If the intended outcome does not occur, try alternative interventions.

are as standardized as possible for all cases. Standardized assessment data provide the means for linking each new case to previous cases on which relations between assessment data and outcomes have been established. To score the empirically based taxa, the CBCL should be obtained from at least one parent or parent-surrogate for every case. The TRF should be obtained for those children who attend school, while the YSR should be obtained from 11- to 18-year-olds.

If the children are interviewed with the SCIC (McConaughy & Achenbach, 1990), syndrome scores analogous to those obtained from the CBCL, TRF, and YSR can be included in the assessment data base. Demographic data, such as the child's age, sex, ethnicity, and SES, can be routinely entered into the data base, as can test data and data on family composition (e.g., both biological parents; single parent; blended family). Developmental history and medical data can be coded for particular risk factors that might affect actuarial findings, such as developmental delays and serious illnesses or handicaps. DSM diagnoses, as well as DSM Axis IV scores for psychosocial stressors and Axis V scores for global assessment of functioning, can also be entered, preferably derived from procedures for which good reliability has been established.

2. Combining Assessment Data. To answer Question 2 about combining assessment data, numerous procedures can be tested for optimizing relations between the assessment data and important outcomes. If the outcome variables are quantitative, multiple regression analyses can be used to identify the combination of assessment variables that best predicts the outcome scores. Examples of quantitative outcome measures include the mean of standardized total problem scores from the CBCL, TRF, and YSR, and DSM Axis V global assessment of functioning scores. If the outcomes are dichotomized (e.g., presence vs. absence of a diagnosis), discriminant analyses can be done to determine which combination of variables best predicts good versus poor outcomes. Other ways of combining data can also be tested, such as comparing outcomes for children initially classified according to syndromes or profile types and scored according to severity, via total problem scores on the CBCL, TRF, or YSR, or DSM Axis V global assessment of functioning scores.

In developing an actuarial system, we should be prepared to test diverse candidate predictors and diverse ways of combining them. However, to correct for the shrinkage in predictive relations that occurs when empirically derived formulas are applied to new samples, the initial formulas must be cross-validated on new samples or on "hold-out" portions of the original sample that are not included in the derivation of the formulas (SAS Institute, 1990).

3. Severity of Problems. To address Question 3 in Table 7-1, actuarial procedures should be used to compare treated and untreated samples of children who have high levels of problems. Because only a portion of children who have high problem levels receive treatment, comparisons can be made in longitudinal studies of large general population samples (e.g., Stanger, Achenbach, & McConaughy, 1993; Verhulst, Eussen, Berden, Sanders-Woudstra, & van der Ende, 1993). Outcomes can then be compared for children who were initially deviant with respect to certain kinds of problems and then received an intervention versus children who had similar problems but did not receive the intervention. If the outcomes are equally good for both groups, this would indicate that intervention as typically rendered may not be warranted for such problems. On the other hand, if particular kinds of problems have poor outcomes even after intervention, this would indicate that better interventions are needed for such problems.

4. Choice of Interventions. To address Question 4, concerning optimal interventions, controlled comparisons are needed to determine which kinds of intervention work best for which problems. There have been numerous controlled studies of interventions for various childhood problems. Meta-analyses have shown that several kinds of intervention can significantly reduce several kinds of problems (Weisz, Weiss, & Donenberg, 1992). However, much remains to be learned about which interventions are likely to be most cost-effective for particular kinds of problems. This requires research that groups children by problem patterns (e.g., according to syndromes or profile types) and then compares the different groups after different interventions. If different interventions are found to be equally effective for particular patterns of problems, then the least costly and most easily implemented interventions are to be preferred.

Unlike the evidence for the efficacy of interventions done under research conditions, the few studies evaluating interventions under more typical clinical conditions have not yielded evidence for efficacy (Weisz et al., 1992). Several factors may contribute to the difference between outcomes found under research versus clinical conditions. Such factors include the less rigorous tests of outcomes, less effective implementation of interventions, and less precise selection of children and therapists for particular interventions under typical clinical conditions then under research conditions. However, because efficacy has been demonstrated under controlled research conditions, it is important to extend the beneficial features of the research conditions to clinical settings. This can be done by classifying children according to syndromes or profile types and then comparing the efficacy of particular interventions for children classified by the syndromes or profiles. If certain interventions are found to be more effective than others for certain syndromes or profile types, then the use of actuarial procedures to assign new cases to the most appropriate interventions should be done within a system that ensures correct implementation of the interventions.

5. Expected Improvement. Considering the early stage of our knowledge about the efficacy of interventions for children's behavioral/emotional problems, it is not surprising that most research has focused on determining whether one intervention reduces problems more than another intervention or no intervention. However, a further issue, raised in Question 5, is whether an intervention can produce large enough benefits at low enough cost and risk to be worth undertaking. When the question of effect size has been addressed in research, the answers have mainly concerned the magnitude of the decline in problems from pre- to post-treatment. This is indeed an important way to evaluate the potential benefit of an intervention. However, it is also important to determine whether children's functioning is likely to remain quite deviant after a particular intervention or whether deviant children will reach the normal range for their age and sex.

To evaluate this aspect of intervention efficacy, pre- to post-intervention comparisons must employ measures that compare a child with normative samples of peers. By using the CBCL, TRF, and/or YSR, it can be determined if children are deviant from their peers with respect to each syndrome prior to intervention and following intervention. Although some interventions may be valuable and cost-effective even if they do not yield functioning in the normal range, those that reduce problems to the normal range are likely to be the most valuable.

6. Duration of Intervention. As evaluations of interventions become more sophisticated and differentiated, Question 6 can be addressed, i.e., how long should a particular intervention continue? If two interventions are equally effective, the shorter one would usually be preferred, because it would probably be completed in more cases and is likely to be less costly.

If interventions are found to be effective in controlled studies, an additional step would be to experiment with shorter or less intense versions to determine the minimum "dose" that is fully effective. On the other hand, some childhood problems, such as those of the Attention Problems and Aggressive Behavior syndromes, and some profile patterns may be especially difficult to change. To be effective, interventions may therefore need to continue in some form for very long periods, or prosthetic aids may need to be provided indefinitely. This is true of many chronic physical disorders, such as diabetes, epilepsy, and asthma, where intervention and avoidance of exacerbating conditions need to continue indefinitely. Despite the need for continued intervention for these disorders, the intervention can be highly successful in enabling people to live normal lives. The social costs of problems such as extreme aggression can be so high that even very long-term or repeated interventions may be cost-effective if they minimize the damage that such problems inflict.

7. Alternative Interventions. Both in the research evaluation of interventions to find the best form of help for particular syndromes and profile types and in the clinical application of interventions to individual children, it is important to continually assess children's functioning. Even if an intervention focuses on only one syndrome, such as Attention Problems, or one profile type, such as the Delinquent-Aggressive type, problems and competencies other than those targeted for change should also be assessed. Otherwise, it may not be recognized that an apparently successful intervention for one syndrome, such as Attention Problems, may be followed by a lack of improvement or even worsening in other areas, such as the Anxious/ Depressed syndrome. By readministering the CBCL, TRF, and/or YSR at intervals of 3 to 6 months, it can be determined whether interventions are followed by changes in areas other than those targeted by the intervention.

If improvement is insufficient despite an adequate trial of a particular intervention, then other interventions that have proven effective with similar problems should be tried. A truly comprehensive actuarial data base would include contingency options for selecting alternatives to the first choice intervention, if that intervention was ineffective after being tried for the full period normally required for good results.

PRACTICAL APPLICATIONS OF SYNDROMES AND PROFILE TYPES

As indicated in the preceding section, improvement of decision-making involves both research and practical applications of empirically based taxa. The actuarial strategy outlined in Table 7-1 provides a bridge between the advancement of generalized knowledge through research and the application of such knowledge to helping the individual child. As research identifies more correlates and expands our theoretical understanding of the syndromes and profile types, actuarial decision-making can become more sophisticated. This, in turn, can improve our ways of helping individual children, especially if practitioners use empirically based taxa according to actuarial principles.

Actuarial approaches to child psychopathology are still in their infancy. Furthermore, the utility of empirically based taxa is not restricted to actuarial systems, as illustrated elsewhere (e.g., Achenbach, 1991b, 1991c, 1991d, 1993b; McConaughy, 1993). Nevertheless, to point the way toward new practical applications, the examples here highlight some ways in which actuarial principles can enhance the practical utility of empirically based taxa. The flow chart in Figure 7-1 illustrates relations between practical decision points and the use of the empirically based taxa.

The specific contents of each box in Figure 7-1 may vary from one setting and case to another. For example, in *Box I*, the TRF would only be obtained for children attending school and the YSR would only be obtained for 11- to 18-year-olds. Other data not listed in the box would be obtained

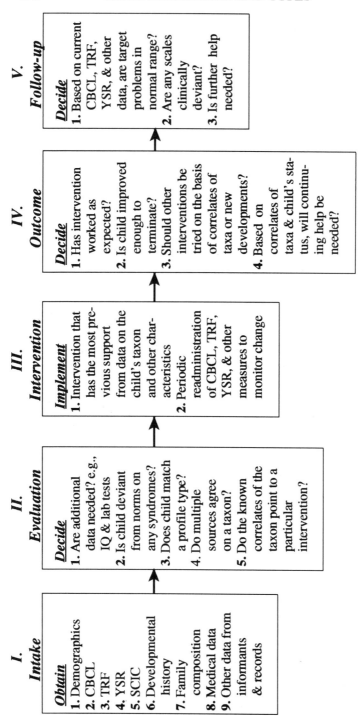

Figure 7-1. Examples of relations between practical decision points and empirically based taxa.

when available and relevant to the particular case. Similarly, evaluation questions will often extend beyond those in *Box II*. Furthermore, the data and decisions are by no means restricted to the child. Family and other variables will always be relevant. The conclusion of the evaluation may be that a marital problem should be the focus of intervention, or that a family systems intervention is warranted, or that a parent should receive individual treatment, or that all of these are needed, whether or not direct intervention with the child is warranted.

If the child is being evaluated in a school context, it is important to consider ways in which the school environment and staff may need changing, as well as the child. Because the possibilities are so diverse, it is not feasible to represent them all simultaneously in a single conceptual scheme. An important aspect of clinical skill is to be able to recognize and deal with the idiosyncrasies that make each case in some respects unique.

Rather than attempting the impossible task of capturing all the idiosyncrasies of each case, empirically based taxonomy and its actuarial applications are intended to capitalize on the common elements of cases. By systematically identifying features shared by cases at the level of syndromes and profile types, and by linking cases to a growing array of correlates, empirically based taxonomy helps us access knowledge that extends well beyond what can be accumulated from any single caseload. At the same time, the standardized scoring of syndromes and profile types from easily obtained informant reports frees the practitioner to concentrate on dealing with the idiosyncratic aspects of cases that are not subject to standardization. Instead of viewing everything about a case as unique, the practitioner can thus distinguish the aspects that can be clearly linked to other cases from those aspects that cannot be so clearly linked to other cases. To improve our ways of helping children, practitioners must be able to access knowledge and methods gleaned from systematic research on many children, as well as applying their own personal skills to the idiosyncrasies of the cases for which they are responsible.

To return now to Figure 7-1, if data from multiple sources agree in indicating deviance on a particular syndrome or in classifying the child according to a profile type, this would provide a focus for intervention and subsequent reassessment to evaluate changes in response to the intervention. For example, if parent-, teacher-, and self-reports all yielded T scores ≥ 67 on the Social Problems syndrome and the child's profile correlated $\geq .445$ with the cross-informant Social Problems type, this would argue for an intervention directed at the problems comprising this syndrome, such as *Acts too young for age, Too dependent, Doesn't get along with other kids, Gets teased, Not liked by other kids*, and *Prefers younger kids*.

As summarized in Chapter 6, the Social Problems syndrome manifests high heritability, stability, and cross-informant agreement. It also discriminates very well between referred and nonreferred children. Even though it has no clear counterpart in the DSM, it is likely to involve pervasive and persistent impairment. Several interventions for poor social skills are available, some of which have yielded evidence for efficacy in controlled studies (reviewed by Hops & Greenwood, 1988; Zaragoza, Vaughn, & McIntosh, 1991). One of these interventions could be selected on the basis of factors such as appropriateness for the child's specific social problems, the child's sex and age, the child's other problems and competencies, and relevant family characteristics.

After the intervention is implemented, the CBCL and other relevant measures can be readministered to monitor change. When the intervention has been completed, the CBCL and other measures can be used to decide whether the child has improved enough to terminate or whether additional intervention efforts are needed. A follow-up assessment (e.g., at 9 months after intake) can be used to determine whether the child is functioning in the normal range with respect to the Social Problems syndrome and whether there is evidence for new problems in other areas. It can then be decided whether further help is needed. Similar approaches can be taken with other problems, although the decision to implement an intervention, the choice of intervention, etc., will depend on the specific problems, other characteristics of the case, and evidence for the efficacy of interventions for the problems in question.

SUMMARY

Because the boundaries between childhood disorders are unclear, research must employ a "bootstrapping" strategy whereby admittedly imperfect procedures are developed to assess imperfectly defined variables. Correlates of the imperfect assessment procedures are then tested and the findings are used to improve the procedures and concepts of variables. This process is repeated further to improve the procedures and variables. Confidence in particular *hypothetical constructs* should increase as *nomological* (lawful) networks of relations to other variables are supported.

This chapter outlined research and practical applications of the empirically based syndromes and profile types. To advance the taxonomy and understanding of child psychopathology, bootstrapping research is needed to progressively improve the definition and assessment of variables and to test their correlates. Longitudinal research is needed to test the developmental course of syndromes and profiles and to identify differences in correlates at different developmental levels. Because the DSM has a pervasive influence on research and clinical thinking, it is important to continue testing the relation of each new version of DSM diagnoses to the empirically based taxa.

An actuarial strategy for improving clinical decision-making can provide an effective bridge between research and practical applications. The actuarial approach bases decisions about individual cases on explicit rules for applying previous empirical findings obtained for large samples of similar cases. There is abundant evidence that the actuarial method often yields more valid decisions than the clinical method of mentally combining data specific to individual cases. The superiority of the actuarial method results from its use of data from more diverse cases than the individual practitioner has seen, its rigor in combining data, its use of empirically verified relations to outcomes, and its consistency in generating decisions in the same way from case to case.

An actuarial strategy can be used to improve applications of empirically based taxonomy to practical decisions about what assessment data to obtain, combining assessment data, deciding whether problems are severe enough to warrant intervention, choosing interventions, specifying expectations for the efficacy of interventions, deciding on the duration of interventions, and choosing alternative interventions. Many practical applications of empirically based taxa have been reported previously, but actuarial principles open up new possibilities for improving decision-making and services by means of empirically based taxonomy.

Chapter 8
Overview and Future Directions

Children's behavioral and emotional problems stem from many causes and take many forms. Some of these problems may have diverse and severe consequences for others as well as for the children themselves. Many people are employed to ameliorate children's problems, but there is insufficient evidence for the efficacy of services as they are typically rendered (Weisz et al., 1992). Furthermore, comparisons of American children at different points in time indicate that problem levels have risen in recent years (Achenbach & Howell, 1993).

Massive increases in costs for health care, special education, and youth services are contributing to pressures for new approaches to helping troubled children. It is therefore incumbent on professionals who work with children to make their efforts more cost-effective, both to improve accountability and to produce outcomes that are as favorable as possible with the available resources. Because efforts to cut costs by managing care are inevitable, it is essential that we preserve and strengthen the most effective kinds of care while eliminating practices that are ineffective, wasteful, or even harmful.

The taxonomic issues considered in this book may seem foreign to some who work with troubled children. However, they have been raised in order to improve our ways of dealing with the everyday tasks of assessing children, selecting optimal interventions, maximizing efficacy, and evaluating outcomes to determine whether additional help is needed. The taxonomic issues are also relevant to improving the administrative classifications that are applied to children for purposes of special education and third party payment, as well as to training practitioners and advancing knowledge through research.

The empirically based syndromes and profile types detailed in this book are scored from rating forms that are now widely used in many settings. The assessment data are obtained at little cost from informants and require little professional time. Even without considering the taxonomic aspects, practitioners can use the assessment data to identify specific problems, clinical deviance on problem and competence scales, and the degree of agreement among multiple informants with respect to individual problem items and scale scores. However, by making use of the taxonomic aspects of the empirically based syndromes and profile types, users can more readily link the assessment of individual children to the growing body of data on these taxa. For example, the data summarized in Chapter 6 indicate differences among the heritabilities, stabilities, and outcomes of the cross-informant syndromes. For syndromes that have the highest heritabilities and stabilities and lead most often to poor outcomes, considerably more resources may be needed to provide effective interventions than for some of the other syndromes. Conversely, for syndromes and profile types that are most responsive to intervention, the optimal interventions should be routinely applied as early as possible.

CURRENT STATUS OF
EMPIRICALLY BASED TAXONOMY

Figure 8-1 provides an overview of the current status of empirically based taxonomy as it has been presented in this book. The topmost box summarizes the basic principles that have guided the derivation of syndromes and profile types thus far. Rather than starting with assumptions about the nature of disorders or the specific disorders that exist, empirically based taxonomy aims to capture the groupings of problems that actually occur in the populations of interest. In order to identify the groupings of problems, standardized

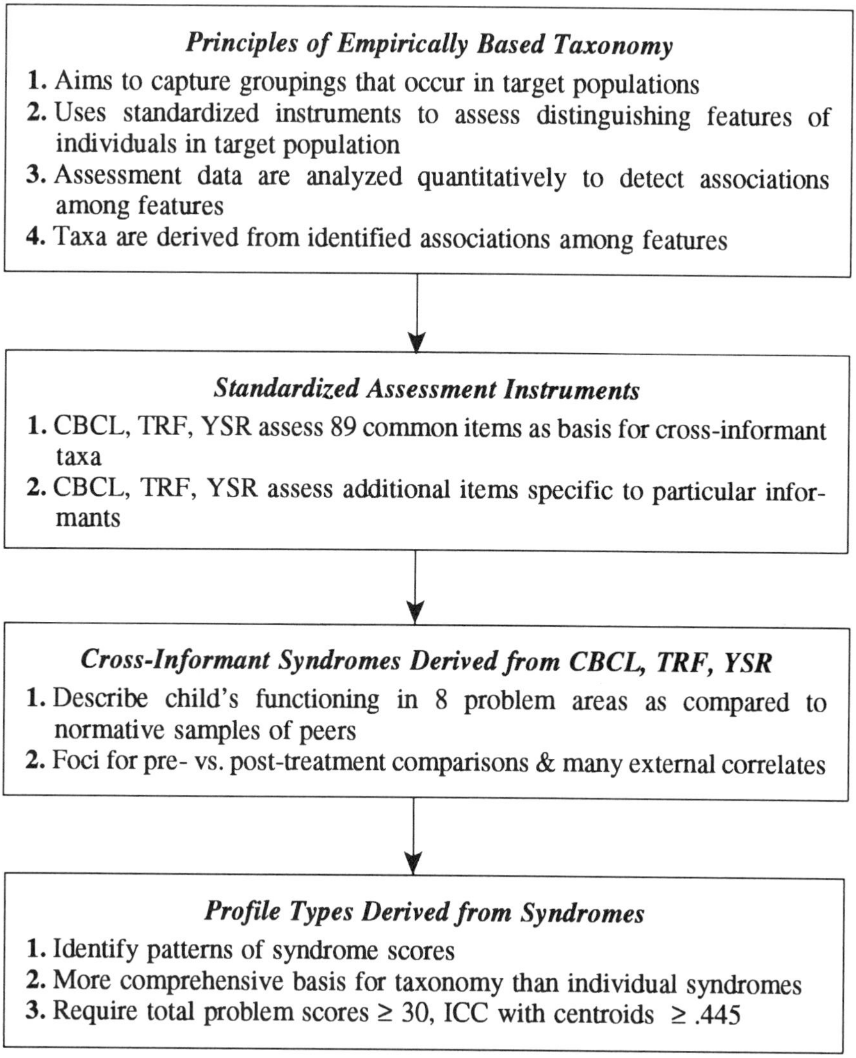

Principles of Empirically Based Taxonomy

1. Aims to capture groupings that occur in target populations
2. Uses standardized instruments to assess distinguishing features of individuals in target population
3. Assessment data are analyzed quantitatively to detect associations among features
4. Taxa are derived from identified associations among features

---

Standardized Assessment Instruments

1. CBCL, TRF, YSR assess 89 common items as basis for cross-informant taxa
2. CBCL, TRF, YSR assess additional items specific to particular informants

---

Cross-Informant Syndromes Derived from CBCL, TRF, YSR

1. Describe child's functioning in 8 problem areas as compared to normative samples of peers
2. Foci for pre- vs. post-treatment comparisons & many external correlates

---

Profile Types Derived from Syndromes

1. Identify patterns of syndrome scores
2. More comprehensive basis for taxonomy than individual syndromes
3. Require total problem scores $\geq$ 30, ICC with centroids $\geq$ .445

Figure 8-1. Main components of current version of empirically based taxonomy.

instruments are used to assess the differentiating features of individuals chosen to represent the range of variation in the target population. Taxa are then derived from quantitative analyses of associations among the features.

The second box in Figure 8-1 summarizes the roles of the instruments that have provided data for the derivation of taxa. After the taxa have been derived, the data obtained on new individuals with these instruments can be used to match the individuals to the previously derived taxa. Although we have focused so far on the CBCL, TRF, and YSR, it may be possible to expand empirically based taxonomy to include data from other sources, such as clinical interviews, tests, and direct observations in settings such as classrooms. It remains to be seen whether these procedures can increase the validity and utility of the existing empirically based taxa in cost-effective ways. If not, these additional procedures would nevertheless add to the comprehensiveness of assessment when they are feasible at reasonable cost. Additional data, such as demographics, medical findings, and family characteristics, will usually be important to obtain even if they are not formally included in a taxonomy.

As indicated in the third box, the cross-informant syndromes can be used to describe children's functioning in terms of eight problem areas. The syndromes provide foci for evaluating outcomes and other correlates. They also provide a taxonomy of sets of co-occurring problems. This level of taxonomy is roughly analogous to the diagnostic categories of the ICD-10 (World Health Organization, 1992) and DSM (American Psychiatric Association, 1993), in the sense that both approaches embody relatively small subsets of similar problems thought to co-occur. Although the syndromes are not necessarily expected to correspond to particular diagnostic categories, several studies reviewed in this book have shown significant relations between DSM categories and the syndromes (e.g., Edelbrock & Costello, 1988; Rey & Morris-Yates, 1992; Weinstein, et al., 1990).

The eight cross-informant syndromes served as the input for the cluster analyses that identified patterns of syndrome scores. In effect, the profile types reflect higher order patterns of co-occurring problems that offer a more comprehensive basis for taxonomy than do individual syndromes. However, unlike the syndromes, which are scorable from all completed CBCLs, TRFs, and YSRs, ICCs with profile types are only computed from forms that have total problem scores ≥ 30. This is to ensure that the differences among a child's syndrome scores are based on enough items to be meaningful. Furthermore, a child's profile is considered to match a type only if it has an ICC $\geq .445$ with the *centroid* of the profile type. (The *centroid* is the set of clinical T scores on the eight syndrome scales that operationally define the type. Note that the printout of a child's computer-scored profile may not look like the centroid that yields the highest ICC with the child's profile. This is because the printout displays the child's syndrome scores in relation to those of the *nonclinical normative* samples, whereas the centroid is defined by T scores derived from *clinical* samples.)

Because the profiles are intended to classify only those children who have at least moderate total problem scores and at least a moderate resemblance to a type, the profile-based taxonomy encompasses fewer children than the syndrome-based taxonomy. However, this is consistent with the aim of distinguishing among patterns of problems where the problems are substantial enough to have meaningful patterns and where the patterns are shared by enough children to warrant comparing their correlates.

As detailed in Chapter 5, users can choose from several ways to classify children who are deviant on individual syndromes. If interventions are to be tested for efficacy, it is important to include subjects who are all clinically deviant on the target syndrome. However, in view of the high rates of comorbidity among most problems (McConaughy & Achenbach, 1993), it is seldom feasible or desirable to exclude all children who are also deviant in other areas. If tests of efficacy include only children whose problems are confined to one area, the children may be so atypical as to provide an insufficient basis for generalizing the findings to more typical children.

The profile types provide an additional way to group children that takes account of relations among syndromes. Although several profile types, such as the Social Problems type, are defined mainly by higher scores on one syndrome than on the other seven, the syndrome peaks are high relative to scores on other syndromes for the clinically referred children on whom the centroids were based. Thus, even those scores of a profile type that are below the mean of the clinical T scores are apt to be higher than scores typically obtained by nonreferred children. By checking the profile types of children chosen by single syndrome scores for tests of treatment efficacy, we can determine how homogeneous they are with respect to their overall profile patterns. If samples are large enough, outcomes can be compared for subjects who are all high on the target syndrome but differ in profile types.

FUTURE DIRECTIONS FOR EMPIRICALLY BASED TAXONOMY

At its current stage of development, empirically based taxonomy provides practical procedures for identifying deviance in terms of syndromes of co-occurring problems and for grouping children according to their profiles of scores on these syndromes. Numerous applications and correlates of the syndromes have been reported (Brown & Achenbach, 1993). The initial analyses of the profile types reported in this book indicate that they, too, will yield many significant findings. Empirically based taxonomy and its underpinnings in empirically based assessment represent a general paradigm for advancing knowledge and ways of dealing with children's behavioral/emotional problems. This paradigm does not constitute a final endpoint but a source of concepts, strategies, and methods to be applied in new ways. Table 8-1 summarizes some future directions for applications and further development of empirically based taxonomy.

Table 8-1
Some Future Directions for Empirically Based Taxonomy

1. Apply research standards for assessment, taxonomy, decision-making, & interventions to clinical services.

2. Apply actuarial principles to decision-making for clinical services & research.

3. Focus research & training on taxonomic tasks needed to improve services.

4. Apply a taxonomic "bootstrapping" strategy to clinical services as well as to research.

5. Test the contributions of other types and sources of assessment data to the improvement of taxonomy and the prediction of outcomes.

6. Test empirically based taxa as markers for different etiological factors.

7. Test intervention efficacy as a function of taxonomic differences.

8. Develop prevention strategies on the basis of findings from 1-7.

The particular directions summarized in Table 8-1 and outlined below primarily concern ways to help troubled children more effectively and ultimately to prevent problems whenever possible. Prevention is a culmination of the other steps, because it requires firm knowledge of relations between etiology, early risk factors, effective interventions, and the application of interventions to populations, only a portion of which are likely to have poor outcomes without intervention.

1. Apply research standards to clinical services. There is compelling evidence that several types of intervention are effective in ameliorating children's behavioral/emotional problems under research conditions, but that these benefits are not being reaped under typical clinical conditions (Weisz et al., 1992). To maximize the efficacy of any interventions, it is important that assessment be done in a rigorous standardized way to identify the target problems, competencies, and other case characteristics needed to select the most appropriate intervention. The assessment data can then be aggregated into the empirically based syndromes and profile types to identify those children who most closely resemble cases that benefitted from a particular treatment in controlled studies. For children who do not resemble cases shown to benefit from any well tested treatment, intervention strategies may require more custom tailoring. However, previous findings on what kinds of interventions have failed, as well as on those that have succeeded with particular classes of problems, should provide guidance even for cases that cannot be closely matched to previous research samples. Furthermore, standardized assessment of the outcomes of all interventions will enable individual clinical settings to accumulate their own data on the efficacy of their interventions.

The typical clinical setting cannot be expected to test efficacy with the rigor of randomized experimental studies. Nevertheless, systematic use of empirically based assessment and taxonomy at intake, coupled with careful matching of interventions to cases and empirically based assessment of outcomes, can document the rates of favorable versus unfavorable outcomes for particular interventions. If certain types of cases and/or interventions have predominantly poor outcomes, this would argue for changes in practice. Conversely, rigorous documentation of good outcomes can provide a basis for applying scarce resources in ways that will be most effective. Because there are so few systematic studies of outcomes under typical clinical conditions, publication of such findings could provide helpful guidelines for other practitioners, as well as identifying targets for more rigorous research.

2. Apply actuarial principles to decision-making. Chapter 7 presented the actuarial approach to decision-making as a bridge between research and practice. Actuarial principles include the following: *(1)* testing relations between assessment data and outcomes over many cases; *(2)* using the findings to construct rules for optimizing the prediction of outcomes from the assessment data; *(3)* applying the rules to new cases; *(4)* testing the accuracy of predictions in new cases; *(5)* revising the rules as needed to improve predictions on the basis of new data. For both clinical services and research, as well as for the application of research findings to practice, actuarial principles prescribe ways of using empirically based assessment and taxonomy to improve decision-making.

3. Focus research on taxonomic tasks needed to improve services. To provide practitioners with clearer, more reliable, and more valid ways of identifying important similarities and differences among cases, taxonomic procedures and concepts need to become more central foci for clinical research and training. The term "taxonomy" itself may seen unfamiliar in relation to mental health services. However, there is a pressing need for training practitioners, researchers, and administrators to share a clearer picture of the important similarities and differences among cases. This would improve communication, application of the most appropriate interventions, knowledge of outcomes and allocation of resources. Empirically based taxonomy is not the only approach to sharpening awareness of taxonomic issues, but its derivation from widely used assessment procedures provides easy access for many researchers and practitioners who might otherwise never consider taxonomic issues.

4. Apply a taxonomic "bootstrapping" strategy. Chapter 7 described a strategy for "lifting ourselves by our own bootstraps" in research efforts to clarify the nature of behavioral/emotional disorders. The bootstrapping strategy entails an iterative sequence of progressively improving the definition and assessment of the variables while strengthening their associations with important correlates. Services, as well as research, can benefit from a strategy of progressively refining assessment procedures, definitions of the variables that they are intended to represent, and their correlates.

As an example, many clinical settings have their own intake questionnaires and interviews for obtaining developmental and family data from parents. It would be desirable to make these procedures more uniform across different settings, although variations may also be needed to take account of differences in caseloads, staffing, intake procedures, etc. Either for application in multiple settings or in a single setting, successive editions of intake questionnaires and interviews can be iteratively tested and modified to improve their efficiency, reliability, cross-informant agreement, and correlations with other variables. Efficiency can be judged in terms of the time, cost, and effort required to obtain the most essential data. Reliability can be tested by readministering the procedures to the same informants on different occasions. Cross-informant agreement can be tested by obtaining data from multiple informants. Correlations with other variables can be tested in relation to other ways of ascertaining similar information, relations to parent and child characteristics, predictive relations to outcomes, etc.

Bootstrapping strategies can also be applied to the iterative improvement of interventions on the basis of findings from outcome assessments. For example, if an intervention produces good results in certain areas, such as the Social Problems syndrome, but not other areas where the same children are often deviant, such as the Anxious/

Depressed syndrome, the intervention could be supplemented to target the Anxious/Depressed syndrome more specifically in addition to Social Problems. Similarly, an intervention that is effective for the Attention Problems syndrome may have to be supplemented to be effective with children who are deviant on the Aggressive Behavior as well as the Attention Problems syndrome.

5. Test the contribution of other data to taxonomy and prediction. As suggested in the preceding section, developmental and family data obtained from parents at intake are potential candidates to be tested for their possible contributions to the prediction of outcomes. These variables, plus others, such as ability and achievement test scores, laboratory tests of attention and biomedical parameters, specific skills, etc., should be tested for their power to identify important taxonomic differences, as well as differences in outcomes under various conditions.

6. Test empirically based taxa as markers for etiological factors. The preceding points have dealt largely with improving services. In addition to the many possibilities for improving services on the basis of current knowledge, further improvements should be possible if more can be learned about the differential etiologies of the groupings of problems identified by empirically based taxa. Such etiologies might include genetic factors, illnesses, stressful events, and harmful childrearing practices, or any combination of these.

In Chapter 6, evidence was cited for different heritabilities of several of the empirically based syndromes. Evidence was also cited for high correlations between scores on the Aggressive Behavior syndrome and indices of low serotonergic activity (Birmaher et al., 1990; Stoff et al., 1987). Although these findings do not prove that biological factors play causal roles in deviance on certain syndromes, they do argue for testing hypotheses about the degree to which biological factors lead to differences in syndrome scores.

7. Test intervention efficacy as a function of taxonomic differences. One of the most needed kinds of research on the efficacy of interventions is to compare the effects of particular interventions on children whose problems correspond to different taxa. Research on the efficacy of interventions has often focused on very specific kinds of problems (e.g., firesetting), on diagnostic categories (e.g., Attention Deficit Hyperactivity Disorder), or on broad classes of problems (e.g., conduct problems). Children selected according to any of these three levels of specification may be quite heterogeneous with respect to other problems and even with respect to the target problems.

There has been relatively little research on the differential efficacy of particular interventions with children who have various combinations of problems. This type of research would be most informative if it compared the effects of multiple types of intervention on multiple patterns in order to test interactions between types of intervention and types of problems. It requires large samples of children from which to select subjects having the appropriate target patterns, plus considerable staff resources to provide different types of intervention. A single study of this type could potentially answer more questions than multiple studies that are not able to test interactions between characteristics of subjects and interventions.

8. Develop prevention strategies on the basis of findings from 1-7. If it can be done, prevention is likely to be far more cost-effective and generally beneficial than trying to undo disorders after they develop. In order to prevent disorders, however, we must first identify the disorders to be prevented. We then need to learn enough about their specific etiologies to know what antecedent variables should be changed. Finally, we need to learn how to change the antecedent variables.

Empirically based taxonomy provides one way of operationally defining differences among disorders as potential targets for prevention. As knowledge about etiology grows, prevention efforts can be tested by seeing whether they can ameliorate etiological factors and whether this, in turn, reduces the rate of problems identified by the taxa or other outcome measures. Prior to more specific knowledge about etiological factors and how to modify them, it is also worth trying to reduce conditions that are generally acknowledged to be inhumane, such as child abuse, whether or not these conditions have any known relation to measures of psychopathology.

SUMMARY

It is incumbent on professionals who work with children to make their efforts as cost-effective as possible. Empirically based taxonomy can contribute to such efforts by improving the evaluation of interventions, the matching of interventions to children's problem patterns, and the advancement of knowledge through more clearly focused research.

This chapter summarized the current status of empirically based taxonomy in terms of the principles that have guided the derivation of syndromes and profile types; the roles of the instruments that have provided data for the derivation of the taxa; the functions of the cross-informant syndromes; and the functions of the profile types.

Future directions for empirically based taxonomy include applying taxonomic research standards to clinical services; applying actuarial principles to decision-making for both clinical services and research; focusing research and training on taxonomic tasks needed to improve services; applying a taxonomic bootstrapping strategy to clinical services and research; testing the contribution of other assessment data to taxonomy and the prediction of outcomes; testing the empirically based taxa as markers for etiological factors; testing intervention efficacies as a function of taxonomic differences; and developing prevention strategies on the basis of taxonomic findings.

REFERENCES

Achenbach, T.M. (1966). The classification of children's psychiatric symptoms: A factor-analytic study. *Psychological Monographs, 80*(No. 615).

Achenbach, T.M. (1985). *Assessment and taxonomy of child and adolescent psychopathology.* Newbury Park, CA: Sage.

Achenbach, T.M. (1990a). *Young Adult Behavior Checklist.* Burlington, VT: University of Vermont Department of Psychiatry.

Achenbach, T.M. (1990b). *Young Adult Self-Report.* Burlington, VT: University of Vermont Department of Psychiatry.

Achenbach, T.M. (1991a). *Integrative guide for the 1991 CBCL/4-18, YSR, and TRF profiles.* Burlington, VT: University of Vermont Department of Psychiatry.

Achenbach, T.M. (1991b). *Manual for the Child Behavior Checklist/4-18 and 1991 Profile.* Burlington, VT: University of Vermont Department of Psychiatry.

Achenbach, T.M. (1991c). *Manual for the Teacher's Report Form and 1991 Profile.* Burlington, VT: University of Vermont Department of Psychiatry.

Achenbach, T.M. (1991d). *Manual for the Youth Self-Report and 1991 Profile.* Burlington, VT: University of Vermont Department of Psychiatry.

Achenbach, T.M. (1992). Developmental psychopathology. In M.E. Lamb & M.H. Bornstein (Eds.), *Developmental psychology: An advanced textbook* (3rd ed.). Hillsdale, NJ: Erlbaum.

Achenbach, T.M. (1993a). Diagnosis, assessment, and comorbidity in psychosocial treatment research. *Journal of Abnormal Child Psychology,* in press.

Achenbach, T.M. (1993b). Implications of multiaxial empirically based assessment for behavior therapy with children. *Behavior Therapy, 24,* 91-116.

Achenbach, T.M., Conners, C.K., Quay, H.C., Verhulst, F.C., & Howell, C.T. (1989). Replication of empirically derived syndromes as a basis for taxonomy of child/adolescent psychopathology. *Journal of Abnormal Child Psychology, 17,* 299-323.

Achenbach, T.M., & Edelbrock, C. (1978). The classification of child psychopathology: A review and analysis of empirical efforts. *Psychological Bulletin, 85,* 1275-1301.

Achenbach, T.M., & Edelbrock, C. (1983). *Manual for the Child Behavior Checklist/4-18 and Revised Child Behavior Profile.* Burlington, VT: University of Vermont Department of Psychiatry.

Achenbach, T.M., & Edelbrock, C. (1986). *Manual for the Teacher's Report Form and Teacher Version of the Child Behavior Profile.* Burlington, VT: University of Vermont Department of Psychiatry.

Achenbach, T.M., & Edelbrock, C. (1987). *Manual for the Youth Self-Report and Profile.* Burlington, VT: University of Vermont Department of Psychiatry.

Achenbach, T.M., & Howell, C.T. (1993). Are American children's problems getting worse? A 13-year comparison. *Journal of the American Academy of Child and Adolescent Psychiatry,* in press.

Achenbach, T.M., & McConaughy, S.H. (1987). *Empirically based assessment of child and adolescent psychopathology: Practical applications.* Newbury Park, CA: Sage.

American Psychiatric Association. (1952, 1968, 1980, 1987, 1993). *Diagnostic and statistical manual of mental disorders* (1st ed., 2nd ed., 3rd ed., 3rd rev. ed., 4th ed.). Washington, D.C.: Author.

Barkley, R.A., Anastopoulous, A.D., Guevremont, D.C., & Fletcher, K.E. (1991). Adolescents with ADHD: Patterns of behavioral adjustment, academic functioning, and treatment utilization. *Journal of the American Academy of Child and Adolescent Psychiatry, 30,* 752-761.

Barkley, R.A., DuPaul, G.J., & McMurray, M.B. (1990). Comprehensive evaluation of Attention Deficit Disorder with and without hyperactivity as defined by research criteria. *Journal of Consulting and Clinical Psychology, 58,* 775-789.

Biederman, J., Newcorn, J., & Sprich, S. (1991). Comorbidity of attention deficit hyperactivity disorder with conduct, depressive, anxiety, and other disorders. *American Journal of Psychiatry, 148,* 564-577.

Bird, H.R., Gould, M.S., & Staghezza, B. (1992). Aggregating data from multiple informants in child psychiatry epidemiological research. *Journal of the American Academy of Child and Adolescent Psychiatry, 31,* 78-85.

Birmaher, B., Stanley, M., Greenhill, L., Twomey, J., Gavrilescu, A., & Rabinovich, H. (1990). Platelet imipramine binding in children and adolescents with impulsive behavior. *Journal of the American Academy of Child and Adolescent Psychiatry, 29,* 914-918.

Brown, J.S., & Achenbach, T.M. (1993). *Bibliography of published studies using the Child Behavior Checklist and related materials: 1993 edition.* Burlington, VT: University of Vermont Department of Psychiatry.

Brown, S.-L., & van Praag, H.M. (1991). *The role of serotonin in psychiatric disorders.* New York: Brunner/Mazel.

Cantor, N., & Genero, N. (1986). Psychiatric diagnosis and natural categorization: A close analogy. In T. Millon & G.L. Klerman (Eds.), *Contemporary directions in psychopathology: Toward the DSM IV.* New York: Guilford Press.

Cantor, N., Smith, E.E., French, R.des., & Mezzich, J. (1980). Psychiatric diagnosis as prototype categorization. *Journal of Abnormal Psychology, 89,* 181-193.

Cohen, N.J., Gotlieb, H., Kershner, J., & Wehrspann, W. (1985). Concurrent validity of the internalizing and externalizing profile patterns of the Achenbach Child Behavior Checklist. *Journal of Consulting and Clinical Psychology, 53,* 724-728.

Compas, B.E., Ey, S., & Grant, K.E. (1993). Taxonomy, assessment, and diagnosis of depression during adolescence. *Psychological Bulletin,* in press.

Conrad, M., & Hammen, C. (1989). Role of maternal depression in perceptions of child maladjustment. *Journal of Consulting and Clinical Psychology, 57,* 663-667.

Cronbach, L.J., & Meehl, P.E. (1955). Construct validity in psychological tests. *Psychological Bulletin, 52,* 281-302.

Cunningham, S.J., McGrath, P.J., Ferguson, H.B., Humphreys, P., Dastous, J., Latter, J., Goodman, J.T., & Firestone, P. (1987). Personality and behavioral characteristics in pediatric migraine. *Headache, 27,* 16-20.

Dawes, R.M., Faust, D., & Meehl, P.E. (1989). Clinical versus actuarial judgment. *Science, 243,* 1668-1674.

Dunn, L.C., & Markwardt, F.C. (1970). *Peabody Individual Achievement Test.* Circle Pines, MN: American Guidance Service.

Edelbrock, C. (1979). Mixture model tests of hierarchical clustering algorithms: The problem of classifying everybody. *Multivariate Behavioral Research, 14,* 367-384.

Edelbrock, C., & Achenbach, T.M. (1980). A typology of Child Behavior Profile patterns: Distribution and correlates for disturbed children aged 6-16. *Journal of Abnormal Child Psychology, 8,* 441-470.

Edelbrock, C., & Costello, A.J. (1988). Convergence between statistically derived behavior problem syndromes and child psychiatric diagnoses. *Journal of Abnormal Child Psychology, 16,* 219-231.

Edelbrock, C., & McLaughlin, B. (1980). Hierarchical cluster analysis using intraclass correlations: A mixture model study. *Multivariate Behavioral Research, 15,* 229-318.

Edelbrock, C., Rende, R., Plomin, R., & Thompson, L.A. (1993). *Genetic and environmental effects on competence and problem behavior in childhood and early adolescence.* Submitted for publication.

Education of the Handicapped Act. (1977). Public Law 94-142. *Federal Register, 42,* p. 42478. Amended in *Federal Register* (1981), *46,* p. 3866.

Eron, L.D., & Huesmann, L.R. (1990). The stability of aggressive behavior—Even unto the third generation. In M. Lewis & S. Miller (Eds.), *Handbook of developmental psychopathology.* New York: Plenum.

Everitt, B. (1974). *Cluster analysis.* London: Heinemann Educational Books.

Faraone, S.V., Biederman, J., Keenan, K., & Tsuang, M.T. (1991). A family genetic study of girls with DSM-III attention deficit disorder. *American Journal of Psychiatry, 148,* 112-117.

Finch, A.J., Lipovsky, J.A., & Casat, C.D. (1989). Anxiety and depression in children and adolescents: Negative affectivity or separate constructs? In P.C. Kendall & D., Watson (Eds.), *Anxiety and depression: Distinctive and overlapping features.* New York: Academic Press.

Freud, A. (1965). *Normality and pathology in childhood.* New York: International Universities Press.

Friedlander, S., Weiss, D.S., & Traylor, J. (1986). Assessing the influence of maternal depression on the validity of the Child Behavior Checklist. *Journal of Abnormal Child Psychology, 14,* 123-133.

Genero, N., & Cantor, N. (1987). Exemplar prototypes and clinical diagnosis: Toward a cognitive economy. *Journal of Social and Clinical Psychology, 5,* 59-78.

Ghodsian-Carpey, J., & Baker, L.A. (1987). Genetic and environmental influences on aggression in 4- to 7-year-old twins. *Aggressive Behavior, 13,* 173-186.

Gottesman, I.I. (1991). *Schizophrenia genesis: The origins of madness.* San Francisco: Freeman.

Gould, M.S., Shaffer, D., Rutter, M., & Sturge, C. (1988). UK/WHO study of ICD-9. In M. Rutter, A.H. Tuma, & I.S. Lann (Eds.), *Assessment and diagnosis in child psychopathology.* New York: Guilford.

Goyette, C.H., Conners, C.K., & Ulrich, R.F. (1978). Normative data on revised Conners Parent and Teacher Rating Scales. *Journal of Abnormal Child Psychology, 6,* 221-236.

Gray, J.A. (1982). *The neuropsychology of anxiety: An inquiry into the function of the septo-hippocampal system.* New York: Oxford University Press.

Gray, J.A. (1987a). Perspectives on anxiety and impulsivity: A commentary. *Journal of Research in Personality, 21,* 493-509.

Gray, J.A. (1987b). *The psychology of fear and stress.* New York: Cambridge University Press.

Grayson, D. (1987). Can categorical and dimensional views of psychiatric illness be distinguished? *British Journal of Psychiatry, 151,* 355-361.

Guzé, S. (1978). Validating criteria for psychiatric diagnosis: The Washington University approach. In M.S. Akiskal & W.L. Webb (Eds.), *Psychiatric diagnosis: Exploration of biological predictors.* New York: Spectrum.

Helzer, J.E., Spitznagel, E.L., & McEvoy, L. (1987). The predictive validity of lay DIS diagnoses in the general population: A comparison with physician examiners. *Archives of General Psychiatry, 44,* 1069-1077.

Henn, F.A., Bardwell, R., & Jenkins, R.L. (1980). Juvenile delinquents revisited. Adult criminal activity. *Archives of General Psychiatry, 37,* 1160-1163.

Herjanic, B., & Reich, W. (1982). Development of a structured psychiatric interview for children: Agreement between child and parent on individual symptoms. *Journal of Abnormal Child Psychology, 10,* 307-24.

Hewitt, L.E., & Jenkins, R.L. (1946). *Fundamental patterns of maladjustment: The dynamics of their origin.* Springfield, IL: State of Illinois.

Hodges, K., Kline, J., Stern, L., Cytryn, L., & McKnew, D. (1982). The development of a child assessment interview for research and clinical use. *Journal of Abnormal Child Psychology, 10,* 173-189.

Hops, H., & Greenwood, C.R. (1988). Social skill deficits. In E.J. Mash & L.G. Terdal (Eds.), *Behavioral assessment of childhood disorders* (2nd ed.). New York: Guilford.

Horowitz, L.M., Post, D.L., French, R.deS., Wallis, K.D., & Siegelman, E.Y. (1981). The prototype as a construct in abnormal psychology: 2. Clarifying disagreement in psychiatric judgments. *Journal of Abnormal Psychology, 90,* 575-585.

Horowitz, L.M., Wright, J.C., Lowenstein, E., & Parad, H.W. (1981). The prototype as a construct in abnormal psychology: 1. A method for deriving prototypes. *Journal of Abnormal Psychology, 90,* 568-574.

Individuals with Disabilities Education Act. (1990). *Public Law* 101-476. 104 Statutes. 1103-1151.

Jenkins, R.L., & Boyer, A. (1968). Types of delinquent behavior and background factors. *International Journal of Social Psychiatry, 14,* 65-76.

Jensen, P.S., Traylor, J., Xenakis, S.N., & Davis, H. (1988). Child psychopathology rating scales and interrater agreement: I. Parents' gender and psychiatric status. *Journal of the American Academy of Child and Adolescent Psychiatry, 27,* 442-450.

Kagan, J., Gibbons, J.L., Johnson, M.O., Reznick, J.S., & Snidman, N. (1990). A temperamental disposition to the state of uncertainty. In J. Rolf, A.S. Masten, D. Cicchetti, K.H. Nuechterlein, & S. Weintraub (Eds.), *Risk and protective factors in the development of psychopathology.* New York: Cambridge University Press.

King, N.J., Ollendick, T.H., & Gullone, E. (1991). Negative affectivity in children and adolescents: Relations between anxiety and depression. *Clinical Psychology Review, 11,* 441-459.

Kovacs, M. (1981). Rating scales to assess depression in school-aged children. *Acta Paedopsychiatrica, 46,* 305-315.

Kovacs, M., Gatsonis, C., Paulauskas, S.L., & Richards, C. (1989). Depressive disorders in childhood. IV. A longitudinal study of comorbidity with and risk for anxiety disorders. *Archives of General Psychiatry, 46,* 776-782.

Kraepelin, E. (1883). *Compendium der Psychiatrie* (1st ed.). Leipzig: Abel.

Loeber, R., & Schmaling, K.B. (1985). Empirical evidence for overt and covert patterns of antisocial conduct problems: A metaanalysis. *Journal of Abnormal Child Psychology, 13,* 337-352.

Mattison, R.E., & Bagnato, S.J. (1987). Empirical measurement of overanxious disorder in boys 8 to 12 years old. *Journal of the American Academy of Child and Adolescent Psychiatry, 26,* 536-540.

McArdle, J., & Mattison, R.E. (1989). Child Behavior Profile types in a general population sample of boys 6 to 11 years old. *Journal of Abnormal Child Psychology, 17,* 597-607.

McConaughy, S.H. (1993). Advances in empirically based assessment of children's behavioral and emotional problems. *School Psychology Review,* in press.

McConaughy, S.H., & Achenbach, T.M. (1990). *Guide for the Semi-structured Clinical Interview for Children Aged 6-11.* Burlington, VT: University of Vermont Department of Psychiatry.

McConaughy, S.H., & Achenbach, T.M. (1993).*Comorbidity of empirically based syndromes in matched general population and clinical samples.* Submitted for publication.

McConaughy, S.H., Achenbach, T.M., & Gent, C.L. (1988). Multiaxial empirically based assessment: Parent, teacher, observational, cognitive, and personality correlates of Child Behavior Profiles for 6-11-year-old boys. *Journal of Abnormal Child Psychology, 16,* 485-509.

McConaughy, S.H., Stanger, C., & Achenbach, T.M. (1992). Three-year course of behavioral/emotional problems in a national sample of 4- to 16-year-olds: I. Agreement among informants. *Journal of the American Academy of Child and Adolescent Psychiatry, 31,* 932-940.

Meehl, P.E., & Golden, R.R. (1982). Taxometric methods. In P.C. Kendall & J.N. Butcher (Eds.), *Handbook of research methods in clinical psychology.* New York: Wiley.

Messick, S. (1989). Validity. In R.L. Linn (Ed.), *Educational measurement* (3rd ed.). New York: American Council on Education, Macmillan.

Mezzich, A.C., Mezzich, J.E., & Coffman, G.A. (1985). Reliability of DSM-III vs. DSM-II in child psychopathology. *Journal of the American Academy of Child Psychiatry, 24,* 273-280.

Miller, L.C. (1967). Louisville Behavior Checklist for males, 6-12 years of age. *Psychological Reports, 21,* 885-896.

Nuechterlein, K.H. (1986). Childhood precursors of adult schizophrenia. *Journal of Child Psychology and Psychiatry, 27,* 133-144.

Peterson, D.R. (1961). Behavior problems of middle childhood. *Journal of Consulting Psychology, 25,* 205-209.

Quay, H.C. (1986). Classification. In H.C. Quay & J.S. Werry (Eds.), *Psychopathological disorders of childhood* (3rd ed.) (pp. 1-42). New York: Wiley.

Quay, H.C. (1993). The psychobiology of undersocialized aggressive conduct disorder. *Development and Psychopathology*, in press.

Quay, H.C., & Peterson, D.R. (1983). *Interim Manual for the Revised Behavior Problem Checklist.* Coral Gables, FL: University of Miami, Applied Social Sciences.

Remschmidt, H. (1988). German study of ICD-9. In M. Rutter, A.H. Tuma, & I.S. Lann (Eds.), *Assessment and diagnosis in child psychopathology.* New York: Guilford.

Rey, J.M., & Morris-Yates, A. (1992). Diagnostic accuracy in adolescents of several depression rating scales extracted from a general purpose behavior checklist. *Journal of Affective Disorders, 26,* 7-16.

Rey, J.M., Plapp, J.M., & Stewart, G.W. (1989). Reliability of psychiatric diagnosis in referred adolescents. *Journal of Child Psychology and Psychiatry, 30,* 879-888.

Reynolds, C.R., & Richmond, B.O. (1978). "What I think and feel": A revised measure of children's manifest anxiety. *Journal of Abnormal Child Psychology, 6,* 271-280.

Richters, J.E. (1992). Depressed mothers as informants about their children: A critical review of the evidence. *Psychological Bulletin, 112,* 485-499.

Richters, J.E., & Pellegrini, D. (1989). Depressed mothers' judgments about their children: An examination of the depression-distortion hypothesis. *Child Development, 60,* 1068-1075.

Robins, L.N. (1985). Epidemiology: Reflections on testing the validity of psychiatric interviews. *Archives of General Psychiatry, 42,* 918-924.

Romesburg, H.C. *Cluster analysis for researchers.* Belmont, CA: Lifetime Learning Publications.

Routh, D.K., & Ernst, A.R. (1984). Somatization disorder in relatives of children and adolescents with functional abdominal pain. *Journal of Pediatric Psychology, 9,* 427-437.

SAS Institute. (1990). *SAS/STAT User's Guide, Release 6.04 Edition.* Cary, NC: SAS Institute.

Sawyer, M.G. (1990). *Childhood behavior problems: Discrepancies between reports from children, parents, and teachers.* Unpublished doctoral dissertation. University of Adelaide, Australia.

Smith, E.E., & Medin, D.L. (1981). *Categories and concepts.* Cambridge, MA: Harvard University Press.

Sneath, P.H.A., & Sokal, R.R. (1973). *Numerical taxonomy: The principles and practice of numerical classification.* San Francisco: W.H. Freeman.

Snook, S.C., & Gorsuch, R.L. (1989). Component analysis versus common factor analysis: A Monte Carlo study. *Psychological Bulletin, 106,* 148-154.

Spitzer, R.L., Davies, M., & Barkley, R.A. (1992). The *DSM-III-R* field trial of disruptive behavior disorders. *Journal of the American Academy of Child and Adolescent Psychiatry, 29,* 690-697.

Stanger, C., Achenbach, T.M., & McConaughy, S.H. (1993). Three-year course of behavioral/emotional problems in a national sample of 4- to 16-year-olds: III. Predictors of signs of disturbance. *Journal of Consulting and Clinical Psychology,* in press.

Stanger, C., Achenbach, T.M., & Verhulst, F.C. (February, 1993). *Accelerated longitudinal research on aggressive and delinquent behavior.* Presented at the Society for Research in Child and Adolescent Psychopathology, Santa Fe, N.M.

Stanger, C., McConaughy, S.H., & Achenbach, T.M. (1992). Three-year course of behavioral/emotional problems in a national sample of 4- to 16-year-olds: II. Predictors of syndromes. *Journal of the American Academy of Child and Adolescent Psychiatry, 31,* 941-950.

Stattin, H., & Magnusson, D. (1989). The role of early aggressive behavior in the frequency, seriousness, and types of later crime. *Journal of Consulting and Clinical Psychology, 57,* 710-718.

Steingard, R., Biederman, J., Doyle, A., & Sprich-Buckminster, S. (1992). Psychiatric comorbidity in attention deficit disorder: Impact on the interpretation of Child Behavior Checklist results. *Journal of the American Academy of Child and Adolescent Psychiatry, 31,* 449-454.

Stoff, D.M., Pollack, L., Vitiello, B., Behar, D., & Bridger, W.H. (1987). Reduction of 3-H-imipramine binding sites on platelets of conduct disordered children. *Neuropsychopharmacology, 1,* 55-62.

Van Den Oord, E.J.C.G., Boomsma, D.I., & Verhulst, F.C. (1993). *Genetic and environmental influences on problem behaviors in international adoptees: Evidence for sibling cooperation.* Submitted for publication.

Vandiver, T., & Sher, K.J. (1991). Temporal stability of the Diagnostic Interview Schedule. *Psychological Assessment, 3,* 277-281.

Velicer, W.F., & Jackson, D.N. (1990a). Component analysis versus common factor analysis: Some issues in selecting an appropriate procedure. *Multivariate Behavioral Research, 25,* 1-28.

Velicer, W.F., & Jackson, D.N. (1990b). Component analysis versus common factor analysis: Some further observations. *Multivariate Behavioral Research, 25,* 97-114.

Verhulst, F.C., Eussen, M.L.J.M., Berden, G.F.M.G., Sanders-Woudstra, J., & van der Ende, J. (1993). Pathways of problem behaviors from childhood to adolescence. *Journal of the American Academy of Child and Adolescent Psychiatry, 32,* 388-396.

Verhulst, F.C., & van der Ende, J. (1992). Six-year stability of parent-reported problem behavior in an epidemiological sample. *Journal of Abnormal Child Psychology, 20,* 595-610.

Walker, J.L., Lahey, B.B., Russo, M.F., Christ, M.A.G., McBurnett, K., Loeber, R., Stouthamer-Loeber, M., & Green, S.M. (1991). Anxiety, inhibition, and conduct disorder in children: I. Relations to social impairment. *Journal of the American Academy of Child and Adolescent Psychiatry, 30,* 187-191.

Walker, L.S., Garber, J., & Greene, J.W. (1991). Somatization symptoms in pediatric abdominal pain patients: Relation to chronicity of abdominal pain and parent somatization. *Journal of Abnormal Child Psychology, 19,* 379-394.

Watkins, J.M., Asarnow, R.F., & Tanguay, P.E. (1988). Symptom development in childhood onset schizophrenia. *Journal of Child Psychology and Psychiatry, 29,* 865-878.

Watson, D.C., & Clark, L.A. (1984). Negative affectivity: The disposition to experience aversive emotional states. *Psychological Bulletin, 96,* 465-490.

Wechsler, D.C. (1974). *Wechsler Intelligence Scale for Children—Revised.* New York: Psychological Corporation.

Wechsler, D.C. (1991). *Wechsler Intelligence Scale for Children—Third edition.* San Antonio, TX: Psychological Corporation.

Weinstein, S.R., Noam, G.G., Grimes, K., Stone, K., & Schwab-Stone, M. (1990). Convergence of DSM-III diagnoses and self-reported symptoms in child and adolescent inpatients. *Journal of the American Academy of Child and Adolescent Psychiatry, 29,* 627-634.

Weisz, J.R., Weiss, B., & Donenberg, G.R. (1992). The lab versus the clinic: Effects of child and adolescent psychotherapy. *American Psychologist, 47,* 1578-1585.

Wells, K.B., Burnam, M.A., Leake, B., & Robins, L.N. (1988). Agreement between face-to-face and telephone administered versions of the depression section of the NIMH Diagnostic Interview Schedule. *Journal of Psychiatric Research, 22,* 207-220.

Wolfe, V.V., Blount, R.L., Finch, A.J., Saylor, C.F., Pallmeyer, T.P., & Carek, D.J. (1987). Negative affectivity in children: A multitrait multimethod investigation. *Journal of Consulting and Clinical Psychology, 55,* 245-250.

World Health Organization. (1992). *Mental disorders: Glossary and guide to their classification in accordance with the Tenth Revision of the International Classification of Diseases* (10th ed.). Geneva: Author.

Zaragoza, N., Vaughn, S., & McIntosh, R. (1991). Social skills interventions and children with behavior problems: A review. *Behavior Disorders, 16,* 260-275.

INDEX